the 7 spheres of a
FRIENDMaker
Building a Business on Friendship

Art Kelly

The 7 Spheres of a FriendMaker

2023 Art Kelly

ISBN 9798366950152

Nashville, TN

Printed in the United States of America

To my best friend
Rebecca

You've taught me everything
I know about friendship.
Every day I grow more into the man
I want to be because of you.
I love you to the moon and back.

To my children
Caleb, Cole, Ella, and Lucy

I dedicate this book to you and your friends.
Keep loving them well.

To my friend and mentor
Dave Sowards

You are Dave Sawyer. Through and through.
Thank you for being a rock to lean on,
a trusted advisor, and my good friend.
I'm grateful for you.

A FEW WORDS FROM MY FRIENDS...

"This book is a great example of how to lead your life. This is not just for business, but for relationships. I have witnessed Art practicing these principles in his life."
Chris G.

"Art has been demonstrating the "FriendMaker" concept in his business, personal life and faith since I've known him. His presentation to my team was fantastic. He brought up ideas and concepts that gave us some conversation points about how to serve our clients better. It also helped us be open to how we can serve each other better. I highly recommend Art to anyone who has a team and is looking for ideas on how to grow together and want to build strong relationships with your clients. I look forward to having him back."
Brent S.

"Art has been a loyal and inviting friend for years since we met through church. When my parents were looking at houses to move to town, he was helpful and patient as they went through the process. Now he is their friend too. Thanks for loving me and my whole family."
Matt T.

"Art was one of the first people I met when I came to Tennessee, little did I know that our friendship would mold and shape me (with Gods guidance and discernment) into the man I am today, I will forever be thankful for this. I love you man."
Jeffrey R.

"Art is a master at making friends! He sees eternal value in every person he encounters. I am grateful to call him my friend."
Randi Lea T.

"I have had the privilege to be friends with Art for many years. I have seen firsthand how he prioritizes relationships and am excited to see how this book helps others do the same."
Amanda K.

"Art is one of the most genuine people that I have met. His care for others comes through in all of his interactions in every facet of life, so it only makes sense that his mindset would cause him to challenge and re-think how business relationships traditionally operate."
Jacob S.

"I have been friends with Art for over 15 years. What he writes about in this book he has been living out for decades. He is commentating on something we are in desperate need of in our current culture, the necessity of friendship in our lives."
Mark S.

"I've had the pleasure of collaborating with Art Kelly and his clients on numerous business deals. The heartbeat of his success is authenticity, sincerity, and developing true friendships aimed at serving well. I'm excited he's letting the rest of us learn from him through his new book! Not only a business necessity, but amazing life lessons for any relationship. "
Lesa C.

"As a human and business woman who values more than just moving up a ladder or making a ton of money, FriendMaker and all it has to teach about business and life speaks to the heart. This book moves us to ask ourselves what we really want out of life and begs that we check our motives as we serve our customers and friends. Am I just looking to get something from my client or am I there to build relationships and facilitate community, while growing my business as I become a friend? Do I value "doing" vs. "being"? And if so, why? These are things you're guaranteed to ask yourself as you read FriendMaker.

If you are looking for a personal, honest, and genuine guide: Art's work tells a story and offers a simple, yet compelling approach to work and life. Period.

This book is where you learn to be the person others trust and want to do business with, from someone who made friends with me…"
Meghan S.

"My relationship with Art goes back almost a decade, I consider him a friend and mentor. What sets him apart is how transparent he's always been with his intentions. Working with them when buying a house was a no-brainer, I knew above anything else I could trust him."
Samuel S.

"We have over 1400 agents here at Benchmark Realty. We host multiple company-wide Mastermind meetings each year to help engage, motivate, educate and inspire our affiliates. We brought Art on as our guest speaker to share his FriendMaker program and our affiliates loved it. Art did a great job keeping things fun and shared very real ideas that we could all understand and implement immediately. It was refreshing, positive and very real. We have since had him back for multiple events both large and small."
Doug A.

"FriendMaker is a game changer for all people. This is not a book just for the business man or woman, but for all people looking to grow their people skills. Learning to listen better, communicate smarter, love better and stay engaged with people in your life…this book has it all. Art Kelly is the real deal and has proven these principles in his own life not just in business but in day-to-day relationships with his friends. He is the epitome of a friend maker."
Lindsey C.

"Art is a man that I have modeled myself off in regards to every relationship I have had over the last 20 years. He understands what's important within a relationship, and I'm thankful for his continued friendship."
Jacob M.

I've watched Art pursue relationships and build friendships for so long now, it's part of his design. He's great at creating a warm space where others feel welcome. It's truly a gift. He doesn't know a stranger. Believe me, he talks to everyone. He remembers people. Checks in on them, reaches out to them, and genuinely cares about their lives and their businesses.

Becoming a FriendMaker will be the best decision you can make for yourself, your business and for your relationships. He's been my best friend for over 27 years, by choice. Because friendship is a decision of the heart. A choice to connect.

So very proud of you babe! Keep making friends.
The Wife

"I love you and everything you do! I'm not a reader - Let me know when the audiobook comes out!"
Brian

TABLE OF CONTENTS

FOREWARD	11
INTRODUCTION	17
HOW TO READ THIS BOOK	21
PART 1: THE CROWN/THE PROBLEM	29
CHAPTER 1: THE PROBLEM WE'VE CREATED	31
PART 2: THE SKIN /THE STORY	37
CHAPTER 2: WHERE DO I BEGIN?	39
CHAPTER 3: THE VALUE OF YOU	47
CHAPTER 4: WARM FIRES	57
PART 3: THE CORE/THE WORKSHOP	69
CHAPTER 5: LEARNING TO ASK FOR HELP	71
CHAPTER 6: THE 7 SPHERES OF A FRIENDMAKER	81
AUTHOR'S NOTE	93
CHAPTER 7: THE SPHERE OF LISTENING	99
CHAPTER 8: THE SPHERE OF LEARNING	109
CHAPTER 9: THE SPHERE OF LIKING	121
CHAPTER 10: THE SPHERE OF LOYALTY	133
CHAPTER 11: THE SPHERE OF LEAPING	145
CHAPTER 12: THE SPHERE OF LEADING	159
CHAPTER 13: THE SPHERE OF LOVING	169
EPILOGUE: BEYOND BUSINESS	181
ACKNOWLEDGEMENTS	189

Foreward

In today's world of business, we are more transactional than ever before. The thought of building a relationship, or even more extreme, a friendship, with someone you would do business with is as rare as finding a diamond in your couch.

The reality is that human connection is paramount to your success and if you are an introvert this can be just downright terrifying. Any personality can win in business so if you are an introvert and you put the principles of the 7 Spheres of a FriendMaker into practice, then you will learn how to go deeper with your existing relationships. If you are an extrovert then you will make more meaningful connections with people than just having several acquaintances. Either way, you must learn to play to your strengths.

The 7 Spheres of a FriendMaker

In the 15+ years that I have known Art Kelly I have always admired his ability to accomplish the impossible: *Doing business with people you are friends with.* Art does this with a servant-leadership approach like I have rarely seen it done.

Most people do not know how to make this happen so they use the phrase "You can't mix friendship and business." Heck, before reading this book I would even say that too so that I could avoid risking the relationship.

The great news for you is that Art has translated this fine art of growing your business with friendship into an easy-to-follow framework that any personality can learn and apply.

You will still need to be intentional. I would even say that you have to be careful with this framework because you can take something this good and manipulate people if you have the wrong intentions with your application of the process. Yep, it's that good!

So, proceed with caution and check your motivations. Relationships matter more than money and you still must sleep at night and look at yourself in the mirror in the morning. The Seven Spheres of a FriendMaker will take the guess-work out of your next steps of building a world class business via friendships.

Chris Campbell
Sales and Coaching Leader

"...but I have called you friends..."
-Jesus of Nazareth

Introduction

In the year 1493, one year after Christopher Columbus discovered what we now know is the Caribbean islands, he happened upon a new, exotic and sweet delicacy, the pineapple. These delicious and unique fruits boomed in popularity as pineapples were brought to the United States and Europe, crowning both meals and doorposts as symbols of both friendship and hospitality. The popular pineapples gained steam throughout the 15th and 16th centuries and even made their way to the tables of European royalty where some pineapples were known to go for as much as $8,000 per fruit! [1,2]

Back in New England, through the giving and receiving of this magnificent fruit, a new tradition formed. Whenever a party or dinner was being thrown by a host, they would often put a pineapple on the front gate or fence of their home as a symbol of welcome to guests stopping by. Thus, the pineapple became a symbol of friendship in the homes of communities all over the New World.

The 7 Spheres of a FriendMaker

Friendship, it turns out, is what this book is all about. Friendship transcends nationality, religion, race, and gender. In our day and age, friendship is needed more than ever. It's needed in our neighborhoods. It's needed in our homes. It's needed in our marriages. And it's needed in our businesses.

So much of our world relies upon the buying and selling of goods, the trading and sharing of services, and the practice of business. This is a book about how to become the kind of person other people want to do business with. It's a book about learning how to re-establish the link between being a businessperson and being a friend to those you serve.

As I was thinking about how to write this book, it occurred to me that the best way to share these principles, or Spheres, of friendship, is to use the symbol of the pineapple. No other symbol better communicates the power of doing life and business in a way that embraces these critical ideas of both hospitality and friendship. As you read the following pages, I encourage you to keep in mind the spirit of friendship that symbolizes what we as a people, a nation, and a community of people in business are to be all about. You will see this symbol throughout this book, and I hope it serves as a reminder of the journey we are on, that of making friends and dwelling in these spheres of friendship.

What I write in FriendMaker is not complex. In fact, these ideas are simple but powerful, and I believe they will help anyone who owns a business learn how to build the right kind of foundation for their work. I hope that as you read, you will remember that what got you into business wasn't just money or profits, power, or prestige, but people. If your business exists to help people, then I would submit to you that authenticity and trust in friendship with those you serve is foundational to all that you do.

Introduction

As you read, I hope you will accept this as my offering of friendship with you as well. This book, in many ways, is just like that pineapple. I want to welcome you into the idea that you can mix business and friendship and that you can give your business as a metaphorical pineapple to everyone your work touches.

How To Read This Book

Every pineapple has basically three parts: The Crown, the Skin, and the Core. As you read this book, it is important to understand that there are three parts: The Problem, The Story, and The FriendMaker Workshop (as illustrated in Fig. 1). This brief explanation of how to read this book should be helpful.

PART ONE: THE CROWN/THE PROBLEM

I begin the book by briefly outlining the crowning "Problem" of practicing business detached from humanity. In this first part, I challenge the modern assumption that it is a bad idea to mix business and friendship. This book seeks to challenge that idea, rearrange a few things about it, and present a way forward that I call "FriendMaking."

Yes, I know. It seems almost juvenile to suggest that the way forward could be so simple. I'll submit to you that not

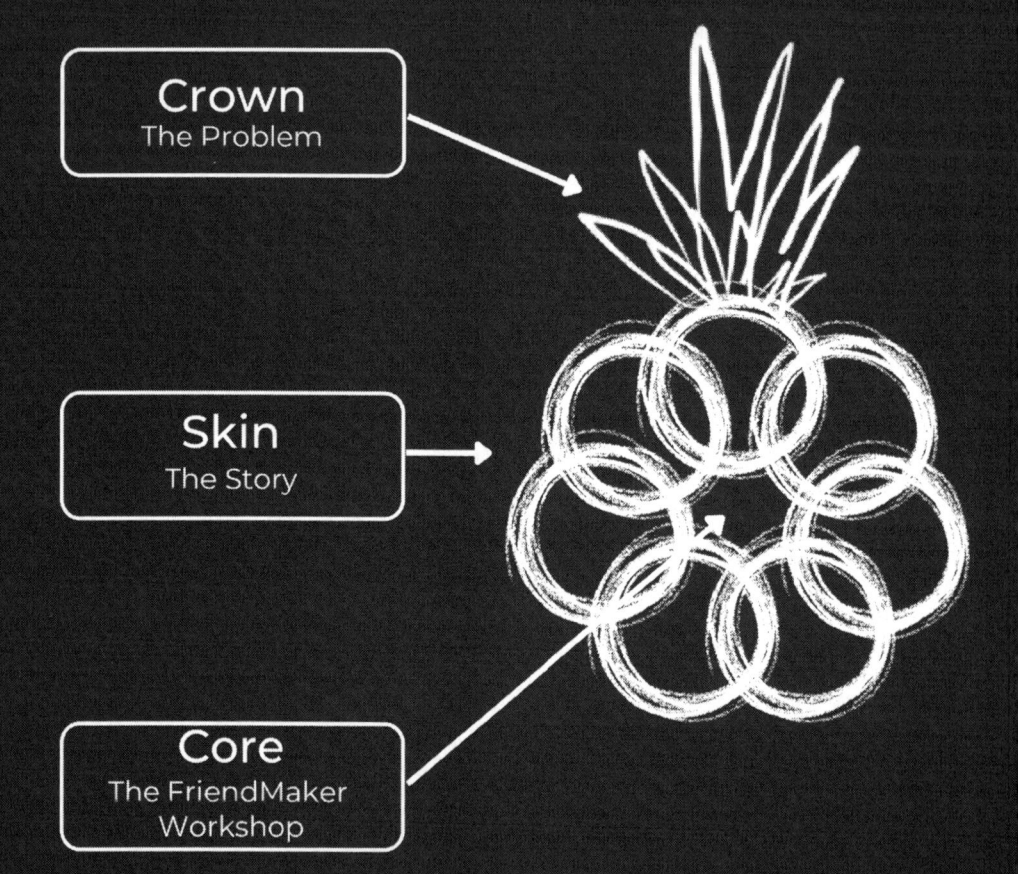

Crown
The Problem

Skin
The Story

Core
The FriendMaker Workshop

Fig. 1

How To Read This Book

only is it possible to mix business and friendship, it is also the best way to do business. The only caveat I have is this: You must become the kind of person who can handle the responsibility of it. This book is a challenge for you to become a person of integrity. It is not popular to hold people to a higher standard. For whatever reason, it seems that it is easier to not care about your clients, to practice business in an impersonal way, and to never risk relationship with those you serve. I hope to be a "voice in the wilderness" of the business world, challenging my fellow businessmen and women to carry the mantle of friendship into their workplaces and create something better with our businesses.

PART TWO: THE SKIN/THE STORY

I've chosen to write this book as a story. I have learned that it is often through story that we learn our greatest lessons. Life comes to us in story form, and sometimes the best way to really gain understanding about complex subjects is through a good story.

The second part of the pineapple, or the "Skin" of this book is the "Story" of Nolan Victor, a middle-aged father and husband who is beginning his journey as a businessman. By using story, I hope to put some flesh on the ideas that will be developed in the workshop section of the book. In the story, Nolan is a real estate agent, but anyone reading his story should be able to draw parallels between Nolan's story and their own entrepreneurial business journey. Any businessperson can use the principles in this book to help them become a FriendMaker in their respective industry.

Though the names and details of the characters in this story have been changed, I modeled Nolan's story after my own. Most of what you will read in this book comes from my own lived experiences, emotions, highs and lows, and successes and failures. This story is deeply personal to me because I have lived it over the past twenty years of trying

The 7 Spheres of a FriendMaker

and failing at various businesses and then ultimately succeeding in my real estate business for the past several years.

The Story will give you a connecting point with Nolan's frustrations and confusion at the beginning of his business journey. But then, Nolan meets a sage-like character who invites him to a workshop that transforms his business and his personal life.

PART THREE: THE CORE/ THE FRIENDMAKER WORKSHOP

Part three is the core of the book. It is the eight-session "Workshop" that Nolan attends to learn how to become a FriendMaker in business. He joins several other business owners who are along for the journey. This is so you can see that the ideas presented in the book are not industry specific, but transferable to a wide range of industries. Real estate was the natural choice for me as the starting point for Nolan because it's what I do for a living. I truly believe the principles of the Seven Spheres of FriendMaking shared by Nolan's coach can be learned and lived by anyone. These principles are reproducible in the lives of the people you have on your team, and they are about teaching something more than just sales skills and items to check off your daily list.

There are plenty of sales strategies and systems designed to help you stay accountable to communicating outwardly with your prospective clients, keep you in touch with your past clients, and provide solid customer service to those you serve. That is not what this book is about. This is a book about being, not necessarily doing. Our culture spends a lot of time, effort, and energy on teaching us how to be more productive. The highest value, it seems, in the business world is not what kind of people we are, but how efficient and productive we are.

How To Read This Book

While we cannot argue with the fact that every business needs to know how to be efficient and productive, I would like to encourage you to consider that it doesn't matter how productive your people are if they aren't becoming better people. It is the opinion of this author that better people make better businesses, not the other way around.

Being Vs Doing

Mike Breen, in his groundbreaking book Building a Discipling Culture, wrote about a rhythm of life illustrated by what he calls "LifeShapes." These LifeShapes are visual illustrations to help us understand the way that life works. With this in mind, I would like to direct your attention to fig 2 - The Semicircle.[3]

As you can see from this graphic, life moves in a rhythm of "being" and "doing." Traditional models of business tend to teach us that our value comes from what we produce or create (i.e. what we do). While there is much value in being able to produce and create goods and services, what matters more is the person we are, our identity. Who we are becoming matters because it is from our identity that our productivity flows. Who we are greatly influences what we do, and that is the main focal point of this book. We must live, or dwell, in spaces where our identity, our character, and our integrity are being developed so that we can be the kind of people we need to be for our families, our clientele, our business partners, and our community.

The arrow pointing to the semicircle is like a pendulum that swings back and forth. After we spend time working on our identity each day, we then swing the pendulum back to our activity. This swinging back and forth between who we are and what we do is meant to be a rhythm of life that we move in and out of. Because our activity needs to flow from who we are, we can keep ourselves from being defined by our activity by intentionally spending time

Be
Identity
Who I Am

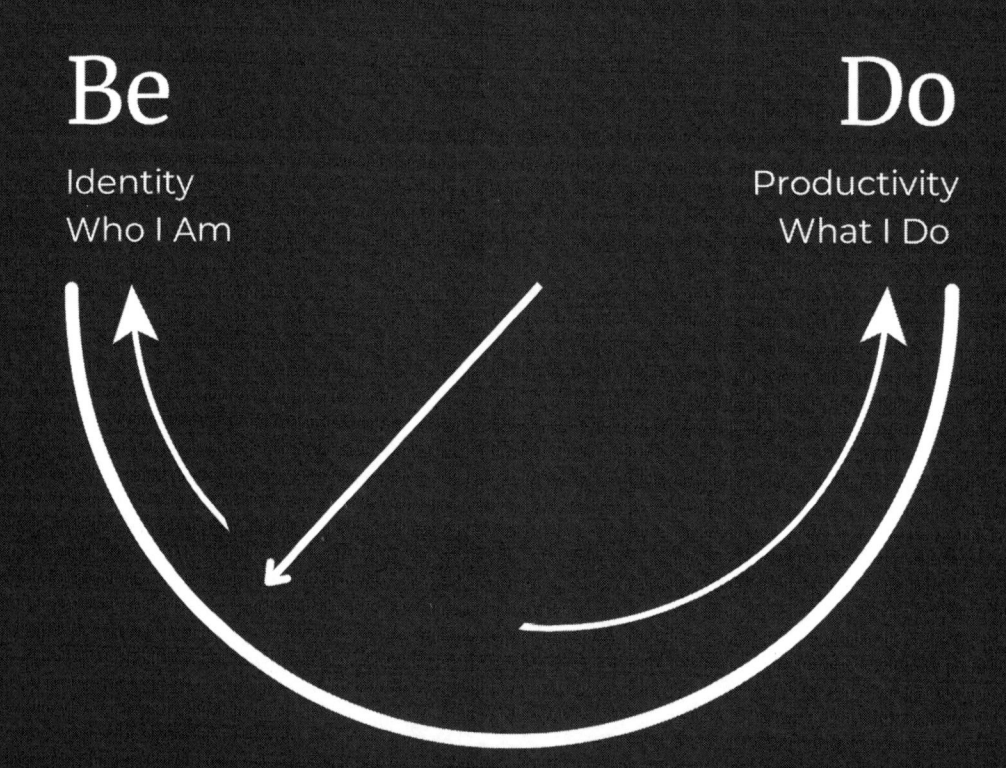

Do
Productivity
What I Do

Fig. 2

How To Read This Book

nurturing, nourishing, cultivating, and curating our inner being. This requires *rest*.

Far too many people in business and in life run themselves ragged trying to prove to all the people in their life who they are by how much they are doing. While it is important for us to create, produce, and act, sometimes it is more important for us to take a step back and reevaluate why we are creating, producing, and acting so much.

This book is about rest. Resting in the Seven Spheres of a FriendMaker. It is in understanding these spheres that you will be able to see how to interact with people so that you can truly put others first and become a FriendMaker.

PART ONE:
THE CROWN/THE PROBLEM

*"You want to know who your friends are?
Start your own business and ask for their support."*[4]
Steve Jobs

"All lasting business is built on friendship."[5]
Alfred A. Antiper

"Never mix business and friendship."[6]
Popular Business Proverb

CHAPTER 1
The Problem We've Created

You've heard it a thousand times: Never mix business and friendship. I've known too many people who have lost some of their closest relationships due to business deals gone sour. Casualty after casualty of businesspeople crashing and burning in their relationships has caused a rift in public opinion about whether you should ever do business with your friends or family. American business magnate John D Rockefeller once said, "A friendship founded on business is better than a business founded on friendship."[7] Whether he meant to or not, by making that statement Rockefeller placed the value of profits above relationship with people.

In the grand scheme of life and business, it seems that the answer to the question, "Is it a good idea to mix business and friendship?" is an emphatic "No!"

But this is a problem. The knee-jerk reaction in the business world to this kind of negative experience has created a gaping hole. So much business done in America now has become impersonal, disconnected, and non-relational for the average consumer. People have gotten used to poor service, diminished quality, and less satisfaction with the purchasing of goods and services. The result is that we distrust salespeople. A vast segment of our population believes that salespeople only want to use them as commodities to get what they want.

Steve Shapiro, the author of Listening for Success, tells us that "most people believe that sales is about getting people to do something that they don't want to do."[8] Because of this definition of what sales is and a lack of awareness of what salespeople actually do, we have a general public that is afraid to trust anyone who bears the name salesman. What's worse, salespeople themselves do not even wish to be called salespeople anymore. Business professionals want to distance themselves from the word "*sales*" because of the negative connotation. The truth is that if you are in business and you are providing goods or services to the public for a price which they have to pay, then you are in sales!

It was Thomas J Watson, the former CEO and chairman of IBM who once said, "Nothing happens until someone sells something."[9] In a nation where consumers spend, on average, $25 billion a day purchasing goods and services, I would say that somebody is in the sales business. And business is good.[10]

This negative attitude toward sales professionals has become a major issue for the average consumer, and many business owners have fallen prey to this attitude as well. Community business owners often don't trust other business owners who provide the same goods and services they provide. They have moved from an environment of healthy competition between businesses to an environment of fear and a scarcity mindset. Many people believe that there isn't enough business out there for all of us. There is fear that they will end up broke and homeless if they do not scrap and fight to keep their piece of the mar-

The Problem We've Created

ket. This causes anxiety, stress, and fear to break in, and it heavily influences much of our modern business practice. As a result, this causes business-people to look to more impersonal means and methods to gain new business.

This has never been more apparent than in the service industries of real estate, mortgage lending, financial advising, and insurance. One doesn't have to look very far in the social media or email marketing world to discover that there are a thousand different companies selling supposed "leads" to willing and impressionable salespeople who feel like they are missing out on the latest business generating gimmicks.

This rise of large corporations that feed on the anxiety, stress, and fear of business owners is evidence that the problem is real and is getting worse. Salespeople are easy fodder for these corporations because they believe that by paying these corporations or social media giants for these leads they will get a good return on their investment. While some may find success with these methods, others get swallowed up by the lead generation machine. What they don't know is that the leads they are paying for are the same leads the other agents down the street are paying for. And the dirty little truth about the leads? They aren't often actually leads. They are impressions, clicks, and inquiries from mostly tire kickers, potential buyers, or just curious consumers. Far too often they are not qualified leads. They have to be converted into qualified leads which requires definite tactics and strategies to convince people to use them as their trusted advisor.

What was once personal has become impersonal. What was once human has become machine. What was once small-town America has become big-box corporate America.

I want to advocate for a different way of obtaining and sustaining business. We haven't mixed business and friendship and look where it's gotten us. This is a large reason why businesses fail. And this is the problem that we face in our current cultural marketplace: There is an over-dependence on impersonal ways and means to get and keep business.

Another Way

FriendMaker is about finding another way. In this book, I challenge the notion that you can't mix business and friendship. I want to suggest that, instead of moving away from people, we begin moving toward them. And we must do it in a way that communicates to them that we don't want to use them as commodities for our own personal gain.

Now, I must admit that many of these ways of obtaining business that I have described do work and I am not debating whether you should use these means to get work. Every business should have a digital footprint, a social media presence, a website, and other kinds of digital marketing strategies. If you want to spend your money on leads, then feel free. It's not wrong to do that.

I am simply suggesting that we stop relying only on impersonal means to develop businesses of personal relationships. Ultimately, when a recession hits or when the economy takes a downturn, the pay-for-leads systems will not be a reliable safety net for entrepreneurs who are in need of sustainable and consistent business. It will be in the relationships that they have or have not developed. Your business will rise or fall on this truth more than any lead generation strategies you may have learned: Whatever you do in business, you must always be in the business of building relationships.

FriendMaker is about building authentic, sustaining relationships with your clients and your strategic partners in the communities where you live. It's about opening your ears and heart to people so that you can serve them better and help them to truly get what they want.

The Problem We've Created

Motivational speaker Zig Ziglar once said, "You can have everything in life you want if you will just help enough other people get what they want."[11] It seems so simple, but it really is true. Help enough people, serve enough people, empower and value enough people in your life, and you will not have to worry about how you are going to take care of your own.

This is not a book about a "secret" or some kind of magic formula that you can put in place to make a million dollars. It is not a promise that the stars will align perfectly for you if you only become friends with people. You must still work hard at your job. People must know that you have the competence and ability to help them get what they want. You must be very good at what you do. Making friends with people doesn't negate the importance of being a skilled professional on every level of your business.

But, before you can practice the work that you do, you have to learn how to become the kind of person that others want to do business with. That is what this book is all about. And it begins with the story of Nolan Victor.

PART TWO:
THE SKIN/THE STORY

*"Story. An epic.
Something hidden in the ancient past.
Something dangerous now unfolding.
Something waiting in the future for us to discover.
Some crucial role for us to play."* [12]
John Eldridge

CHAPTER 2
Where Do I Begin?

Where do I begin? thought Nolan as he stared at the piece of paper in front of him. The state seal at the top of the page confirmed it. He was officially a licensed businessman. After three months of classes, a grueling test, and a few sit-down interviews with different real estate brokers in his community, Nolan Victor finally had his license and was ready to begin.

There was so much information about how to become a good real estate agent, and he had already spent almost three thousand dollars on the front end to get to this point. Now he sat in his car, completely ignorant of what to do next. His new broker, Region's Best Realty, had a great training program for new agents and theirs was one of the most successful brokerages in the community. The best names in the business came out of Region's Best, but he still felt like somebody had dropped a pile of LEGOs™ in his lap and told him, "Go make this contraption!" without giving him the instruction manual.

The 7 Spheres of a FriendMaker

He had all the pieces. He had a brokerage to fly his flag under. His business cards with Region's Best were on order. He had his real estate license. He was a member of his local association. Now he just needed the instruction manual. He needed a roadmap.

Looking around though, he just couldn't seem to get there. The world of business was full of noise and lots of advice. Everywhere he looked, Nolan found information on everything from how to purchase leads to getting coaching (which was too expensive for anyone just starting out), to how to negotiate the deal. The list of subjects in real estate was long and exhaustive, not to mention exhausting!

There were real estate gurus who spoke at national conferences about how to generate your own leads, how to create a digital footprint, how to advertise your business to stand out above the crowd, how to build a business by referrals, how to recession-proof your business...you name it! If it could be talked about, there was an industry expert that could give him the keys to success. Somewhere out there, it seemed, there was a silver bullet: a magical formula that Nolan could put into practice that would propel him and his business to the top.

But finding an instruction manual on where to start and how to begin putting the proper practices into place was so difficult to do. And he was left questioning, *Where do I begin?*

The Dilemma

It was about this time that Nolan ran into Scott Rich. Scott had been the top-selling agent at Region's Best Realty for the last five years. With consistently over seventy-five contracts a year his first five years in the business, Scott was the featured speaker at this year's State Realty Conference. It seemed that everything Scott touched turned to gold! Nolan quickly composed himself as Scott pulled up to the office in his brand new, all black Tesla Model 3. It was sleek. Scott was sleek. Nolan felt, well... not sleek. Nolan knew this guy was way out of his league.

Scott got out of his car, grabbed a folder of something important, and walked into the office. Nolan knew Scott--with his sunglasses still on and his custom fit leisure suit--wouldn't give him the time of day. He was always busy handling some new contract from some connection he had. No time for the common real estate agent. He was a rock star.

Besides, it was cold calling hour this morning where the few and the proud new agents hopped on the company's phones and tried cold calling real estate leads for an hour in hopes that they could get an appointment and grab up some business to get something on the map.

"Scott Rich has long since paid his dues on this stuff, I'm sure," Nolan murmured to himself. "Now he's tromping all over the globe, living the good life."

Every once in a while, Nolan would catch a glimpse of Scott's life on social media. Most of the time, Scott was off with his gorgeous wife on some exotic vacation in Africa, Maui, or some island in the Caribbean. Today, he just happened to be in town working on something with his brokers at Region's Best. Scott was young, maybe twenty-seven. *How is it that somebody that young can get to be so successful?* thought Nolan.

Little did he know, he was about to find out.

The Brokerage

Bursting out of the broker's office in a fitful rage, Scott Rich stomped out not five minutes after he had pulled in.

The 7 Spheres of a FriendMaker

He yelled out something about his father and hopped into his Tesla and, with a quiet screech, zoomed out of the parking lot.

Nolan and the two other agents in the office looked at each other. Their brokers, Al and Jane, stepped out of the office and both looked blankly out the window into the parking lot. "There goes our star agent," said Al under his breath. Jane, his wife and co-broker, sighed a heavy sigh and walked back into their office. Something big had just happened, but Nolan had no idea what it was.

Al and Jane were great folks. They had built a business of great magnitude in their community from the ground up forty years ago. They were some of the best agents in town, and Nolan knew he had a good place to get his start. The only problem with Al and Jane, he found, was that though they had been successful in business, they had struggled as a brokerage to maintain people because they just weren't great teachers.

They were good at doing business. They knew how to operate the transactions and get people from contract to close with little to no problems. Even though every real estate transaction is different, Al and Jane had somehow managed to streamline the experience for their clients and that was what had attracted Nolan and many other agents to their business. They had great resources and marketing materials for their agents, and they really did care about the success of their office. But Al and Jane suffered from what many successful businesspeople suffer from: They had an inability to pass on the knowledge they had gained in business through practical teaching or hands-on coaching. They were happy when some people took to the business naturally but didn't really know how to teach or train the other agents how to get their boat in the water and start paddling without sinking the ship.

Where Do I Begin?

The Bistro

Nolan finished up his cold calls from the list the brokers had given him and decided it was time to take a mid-morning coffee break at The Bistro. The Bistro was a local coffee shop Nolan liked to frequent due to its quiet atmosphere and inexpensive but tasty coffee. Nolan often worked on his social media profile and sent out his weekly *"If you need someone to help you buy or sell a home, give me a call"* real estate pitch online. (By the way, those posts hardly ever work, but an agent can spend an hour on social media sites posting and interacting with their online contacts thinking he or she is really working.) Sometimes it worked, but most of the time, Nolan found out later, social media methods have to be much more unique and skillfully crafted than just putting out a request for people to use your services.

A few minutes after he walked in the door, Fran Lee, one of the agents in his office, came in and sat down across the room from him. Fran was a peach. She knew everyone in town and was on the leaderboard of their office, but there was something very different about Fran's way of doing things that Nolan had always liked. She waved and came over to Nolan's table while waiting for her coffee. "Hey, Nolan, how's it going, friend?"

"It's great Fran, I'm just working on some of my digital footprint stuff. Got to get the word out about what I'm doing in this city, right?" The new wave of social media advertising methods had really captured Nolan's attention. Everyone was doing it. He figured he'd better hop on the bandwagon before he missed out.

"That's a great place to start, Nolan! Back when I started in the business twenty-five years ago, we didn't have stuff like the internet and social media. What I could have done back then with the tech we have now! You keep doing what you're doing... some things are different now, but some things stay the same."

The 7 Spheres of a FriendMaker

He wondered what she meant by that. Fran was reminiscing, but then she got really serious. "I'm sure you saw what happened at the office a little bit ago. I'm sorry you had to see that. It's been a long time coming, and I want you to know that I think it's probably for the best."

"What happened, Fran? I've never seen Scott so angry," said Nolan.

"Well, what a lot of people don't know about Scotty Rich is that his uncle is president of Region One Mortgage here in town. For years, Scott has kept his relationship with his uncle under lock and key, but most of his business for the past five years has come from his uncle's business dealings. Because Region One is the largest local lender here in town, it's been around for a long time, and because it's well connected with the city's leaders, builders, and other community officials, Scotty has had a steady stream of business coming to him from his uncle. Evidently something has changed in his uncle's office that has him quite upset."

Nolan found himself a little relieved as he heard this from Fran. Fran quickly and quietly said, "I've said too much. Forgive me, I'm not a gossip, I promise! I just wanted to encourage you as a new agent to not let folks like Scotty intimidate you. Sometimes people swoop into this business and build an empire quickly, but it's not always sustainable. Especially if they haven't done the most important things first."

With that, Fran heard the barista call her name. With a quick, "Good luck!" she sauntered back to her side of the coffee shop and sat down with an older gentleman in a baseball cap and an old jean jacket. He recognized the man as Dave Sawyer, a well-known businessman in town.

Nolan didn't know how to process what he'd just heard. The question that had been rolling around in his mind about rapid successes in this industry was quickly finding

Where Do I Begin?

its answer in Scott Rich. It seemed that Scott Rich's success was not exactly as great as it looked from a distance. He had encountered people like Scott his entire life. He had always wondered about those people who seemed to be exceptionally successful in business and why it seemed that so few had ever reached the top of their industry. He was beginning to wonder if that would ever be his story. Nonetheless, Nolan had learned a valuable lesson from this interaction with Fran:

Success is more than a quick rise to the top.

CHAPTER 3
The Value of You

The next morning Nolan woke up in a cold sweat. The woman quietly sleeping next to him was even more beautiful to him today than the day they had gotten married fifteen years ago. His three children were all nestled in bed and still out like a light. He squinted at his digital clock on the bedside table, trying to see the time. It was 3:00 a.m. Great! A few hours of sleep left and here he was, waking up before his alarm and anxious about life, business, family, and everything else. What was he going to do? With no real plan for success, no idea of what to do to get the business he so deeply desired, and no roadmap to get there, Nolan felt the anxiety beginning to rise.

He got up, put his pajama pants back on, and tiptoed downstairs to the kitchen to start a pot of coffee. He had had a few moments like this throughout his life, but now, at thirty-nine years of age, he felt like things should be better. His family was getting older, and his wife was exhausted from years of running the baking business that provided extra funds for them when they needed it. Nolan

The 7 Spheres of a FriendMaker

longed for her to do the work she loved, not to simply pay the light bill, but to do it because that's what she loved to do.

In the back of his mind, he thought about how reckless it had been for him to take what little money they had in savings and use it to pursue a career in real estate. What had he been thinking? Both he and his wife were now self-employed. They had little business know-how and even smaller savings than they had before he got into this business. With little more than a hope and a prayer, they had thrown all their eggs into this basket. Were they fools? Was there a more sensible way to do all of this? What if he didn't start selling?

These were the questions that woke him up in a cold sweat. These were the questions that rolled around in his mind throughout the day as he attended meeting after meeting, sales training after sales training, only to find that he was more skilled at listening to people drone on about the importance of cold calling, door-knocking, and holding open houses to get new business.

No doubt there was value to all of these "old-school" methods of getting people to use his services. *But there has to be something more...* Nolan thought to himself. *Am I to just resign myself to a life of spending my weekends away from those I love to sit in empty houses hoping someone comes by and needs me to help them buy a home?*

And then there was the conversation he had always had with people who were older than him about "paying your dues" early on so you can do the things you want to do later in life. Nolan had heard this line of thinking his whole life. It was the mentality of "just show up for work every day, work hard, be consistent, and then someone will take notice and offer you a better opportunity."

Nolan knew that hard work was very important. He had

The Value of You

been a hard worker all his life. Whenever it was necessary to take an odd job or swing the night shift or run the early morning truck route to make ends meet, Nolan knew how to do that. But hard work, he soon came to realize, isn't always enough to move forward in life and work towards being able to do more, be more, and have more. That was what life was all about anyway, wasn't it? Doing more, being more, and having more?

Anyway, he knew in his heart, *there must be more than this.*

He woke up his kids and got them ready for school, and they all piled into the van. It was starting to get cold. Nolan knew that winter was not the time to start in the real estate business. Who was going to buy homes this time of year? He dreaded going into the office that day. Nothing more to look forward to than seeing a bunch of people who were doing really well in business stand up and talk about the importance of making those phone calls and getting those appointments. "That's easy for them to say," he scoffed. "I don't even know who to call, what to say, or what to ask them for!"

Making Friends

After dropping the kids off at school, Nolan made his way over to the office on the other side of town. He really didn't want to go to the sales meeting today. He made a U-turn and headed back over to The Bistro. As he pulled into the parking lot, he saw Fran walking in the front door. As she entered, a young lady asked Fran what she did. Fran's response took Nolan off-guard. "Well, I'm a professional FriendMaker!" Nolan laughed to himself. He had never heard anyone describe themselves that way. Curiously though, it resonated with him.

As the line inched closer to the register, Nolan tapped Fran on the shoulder. She quickly turned her head as though he had startled her. Relieved, she said, Oh, Nolan!

The 7 Spheres of a FriendMaker

You scared me! Ha. I'm just all frazzled this morning. So much to do and it seems like things just keep piling up! The morning sales meeting I'm late for, a home inspection at 11:00, a lunch appointment, a closing at 2:00, and back-to-back showings all afternoon! How are you this morning?"

Nolan nodded his head. "I'm great!" he lied and then skirted, "And I understand. Life can get pretty intense sometimes." In the back of his mind, he wondered if that would ever happen to him. A day like Fran was going to have sounded like it would be great for him right now. It would be great to be so busy to have clients falling out of his ears like Fran! He pushed into the conversation a little bit. "I overheard you talking to that girl. Something you said really stood out for me, Fran. When she asked you what you do for a living, you said you were a professional FriendMaker. Not in real estate anymore, I guess?"

Fran laughed. "Oh my, young man. I got out of selling real estate years ago! All I do is make friends for a living and then sell houses to them when the time comes. Didn't you know that's what we do?" The ease with which she said it made him jealous that he hadn't come up with a good pitch like hers just yet.

"Listen, Nolan, you can use that line any time you need to. It's true. But don't think that I came up with that all by myself. There's a whole way of being that I learned from one of the most admired and respected gentlemen in this community. He's a business and life coach and he taught me everything I know about making friends the foundation of my business." Reaching into her purse, she slipped him a yellow card that featured the face of Dave Sawyer.

The card was simple yet impressive. The word "FriendMaker" was emblazoned on the back of the card. The picture on the front was a plainclothes fellow who wore a jean jacket and slacks with a flannel underneath.

The Value of You

Nolan suddenly realized where he knew the guy from. He'd seen Dave meeting with Fran at the coffee shop just a few days ago. He had also seen him at the real estate office talking with his broker when Nolan had first joined the brokerage six months ago. Dave Sawyer was an established businessman, a real estate investor, and well known around the city for all the amazing things he had done to serve the community.

The barista was staring impatiently at both of them by now. Fran stepped to the side and told Nolan to order whatever he wanted, the coffee was on her this morning.

The Value of You

Nolan felt a little bit ashamed for not going to the sales meeting that morning. There were always some insightful bits of wisdom the other realtors in the office and the brokers had to share. But lately it felt like the same old, same old.

That brief conversation with Fran at The Bistro was a welcome relief. She sat down at his table for a few minutes as Nolan began to share his deepest struggles, fears, and anxieties about selling real estate.

"When people ask me, 'How's the market?' I never know what to say," Nolan complained. "I always just try to say that it seems like it's still busy and going good, but then in the back of my mind I really don't even know what that means!"

Fran smiled widely. "If there's one question that people use when they talk to realtors because they don't really know how else to carry on a conversation, it's that one! 'How's the market?' along with 'How's business?' and 'Man, this market sure is saturated with agents, huh?' are all questions that, while they do affect you in some ways, really have little to do with how you are doing as a real estate agent. Markets rise and fall, agents come and go,

The 7 Spheres of a FriendMaker

but there is one resource that is always renewable." His curiosity was now at an all-time high. Fran continued, "One resource you have that doesn't have to have a down quarter and is more valuable than any economic forecast that Wall Street can drum up for you is right within your grasp. Do you know what that resource is, Nolan?"

He thought for a minute but knew that it was probably some winsome marketing strategy that he had not yet heard about. "Grit? Hustle? The Internet?" Nolan said jokingly. Honestly, he had no idea what she was getting at, and he was taking his best stab at the vast world of marketing strategies he'd read about from all the real estate gurus.

"No, ha! Those are all great answers! But the answer, Nolan, is *you*, just simply y-o-u.

"You see, *you* are the resource that is more valuable than any economic forecast, marketing strategy, or sales gimmick learned at the latest conference.

"People in your city need you to bring the full capability of who you are into every relationship that you make in your city. Your past clients need you to be a friend and to stay in touch with them. Your business partners need your friendship to help them wave the banner of their business across the community. Your family needs you to be 100% present with them when you are home, not worried about the market you cannot control or the transactions you are presently dealing with.

"You, not your strategies, tricks, or manipulations, are the resource you need.

"And the way you bring yourself into the lives of the people around you is a very simple thing. It's something that virtually no one is teaching, but I think may be the most important strategy ever." Fran paused. She thought carefully about her next words.

The Value of You

Nolan was a sponge, soaking in everything she had just said, waiting on her next word. "What's the very simple thing?" Nolan asked inquisitively.

Fran opened her mouth and shut it again. Then she began, "Nolan, I want to tell you, but you won't believe me. I think you really need to just sit down with Dave. He keeps his schedule surprisingly open, and I think it would be better for you to hear it directly from him."

"You're killin' me, Fran. You have dangled the carrot of this 'simple' strategy in front of me and now I'm salivating! Are you seriously going to leave me hanging like this?" Nolan smiled nervously. He had really enjoyed this conversation so far. And it felt like it was coming to an end before it should.

Dave Sawyer

They had been talking for ten minutes already, and Nolan could tell Fran needed to go. Her coffee was getting cold! Fran smiled back. Just then, Dave Sawyer walked in to The Bistro. Perfect timing. Fran immediately waved him over. "Dave! I have got to introduce you to someone." Dave, wearing his signature jean jacket & West Virginia University baseball cap, slowly made his way over, stopping to smile and shaking hands with several people as he entered the cafe. Did everybody know this guy?

"Dave, I'd like for you to meet Nolan Victor, a very dear friend and co-worker at my office. We were just talking about you, Dave. Were your ears ringing?" Dave laughed. Nolan chuckled. It was a good moment.

"Why yes, Fran, my ears were ringing. I've heard about you, Nolan. Your wife catered my daughter's wedding a couple of years ago. My, how delicious those macaroons were!"

Nolan had forgotten how many folks his wife had served

over the past few years as she had shared her baked goods with people all over the city. "Yes, she is amazing! I don't know what I'd ever do if we didn't have her cooking our meals every day!"

Fran kindly interrupted them. "Nolan and I were just talking about the most valuable resource he has in his real estate business. I was just about to give him the secret ingredient when I thought... he really just needs to talk to you! Nolan, I'm so sorry, but I've really got to go. See if Dave can set you up for an appointment so you can talk about this together!" With that, Fran darted out the door with her cup of coffee.

Dave quickly sat down and started asking Nolan some questions about his life, his family, and his business. After a few minutes of getting to know each other, Dave said, "Nolan, I'd love to sit down with you sometime and talk more about what Fran was talking about, but I've got someone meeting me here in two minutes. Let me give you something to think about. Has Fran told you about your most important resource yet?"

Nolan nodded. "Yes, I thought she was building up to something big and then she just said... 'It's *you*.'"

"Well, Nolan, she's right. That's the first step in understanding the foundation of building a sustainable business. And I know we talked about a secret ingredient. But actually, the secret ingredient is really not a secret and it's not an ingredient." He smiled.

Nolan could sense a warmth coming from this man that he hadn't really experienced from anyone in business before. "Nolan... I'm going to leave you with this one thought. It is the core of my business philosophy and has been for thirty years. I've owned businesses, run large corporations, had hundreds of employees, and led my own non-profits for years. I was on the elder board of my church for ten years, raised four girls, and have been married for

The Value of You

forty-two years. What I'm about to tell you will change your life if you really grasp it. We can talk more specifics later. But here it is... are you ready?"

Nolan had his pen out.

Dave paused briefly and calmly breathed out a single word. *"Friendship*... the foundation of everything in life that's worth doing and doing well is this simple idea of friendship. I do business with my friends who in turn do business with and refer business to me. I don't make friends to get business. *I get business because I make friends."*

Friendship? This really all seemed too simple for Nolan. It wasn't the "business-y" kind of thing he'd heard at all the conferences. Most of the speakers and folks he'd learned from were so distant and so business-like, he had not thought that something so simple could really be the answer to his struggle.

Dave got up, shook Nolan's hand and slipped him a card. "What is it that you really want in life, Nolan? The answer to that question deserves another conversation. I'm available Thursday next week. I'll block out two hours for you if you've got the time. Let's meet at the Carlton Hotel at the city gateway."

Nolan's head was spinning. He quickly recovered, thanked Dave for his time, and told him he could meet on Thursday.

Dave quickly pulled out a little lined notebook and wrote something down. Everything about this guy seemed so old school, but Nolan was impressed. They parted ways, and Nolan headed back out to his car.

After Dave left, Nolan pulled out his own computer and wrote in his notes, "What do I really want in life?" He didn't think anyone had ever actually asked him that question, at

The 7 Spheres of a FriendMaker

least not the way Dave asked it. He seemed so... well, genuine.

What does this all need to look like? How was he going to bring himself to such a vulnerable spot in business with people? Wouldn't they see right through him? Wasn't this a little bit too childish to be thought of as a strategy? Should he even mix the ideas of business and friendship? Doesn't that always work out badly? And how in the heck am I supposed to answer the question 'What do I want?'

He would soon find out.

CHAPTER 4
Warm Fires

What do I want? That question had haunted him ever since Dave asked it Tuesday morning at the coffee shop. It was now Thursday morning and Nolan had been pondering the question for over a day. He was stuck and he knew it.

On his way to The Carlton, he went by the store to get himself a notebook. This was not his usual mode of operation. The last few years of digital technology had consumed him. He had a smart phone, a smart watch, and an electronic tablet. He took all his notes on his phone. His digital calendar was his only way to operate a schedule, and it seemed to work for him.

But this morning he found himself in the store searching for a notebook he could actually write in. The cashier smiled at him. He noticed it. She was a kind, older lady he had seen there many times before. He struck up a conversation with her, asked her how her day was going. "Long and boring so far, and I've only been here an hour!" she said.

The 7 Spheres of a FriendMaker

"Well, you keep smiling like that and it'll brighten up a lot of people today. Keep up the good work!" Nolan encouraged. With that, he grabbed his items and walked out the door, leaving her smiling from ear to ear. Walking to his car, he felt good about that interaction.

What I really want in life is to make people's day, just like that. The thought came at him as quick as a flash. He pulled out his new notebook and wrote that thought down. He smiled as he sat in his car. This was who he was. He really cared about people. He really wanted people to experience something good when they came across him. He really wanted to do more than just survive in a job. He pondered this for a few minutes and then a flood of things began to flow out of his mind through his pen onto the page.

He began to write:

I want to give more.

I want to create more experiences and memories with my family.

I want to go deeper in my relationship with my wife.

I want my kids to remember that they had a great relationship with me.

I want to be debt free and financially independent, so we can be able to do more than we've ever been able to do before.

I want to make an impact in the world around me by using my gifts and skills to make a difference.

His hand started to cramp. Typing out his thoughts was much easier than writing them out longhand, but he kept at it. For the first time in a long time he felt like he had permission to dream again. Permission that had escaped him from years and years of just doing what had to be done to survive. He didn't want to simply survive anymore. He really wanted to thrive.

Life is short, he thought, *I don't want to waste another minute.*

His 10:00 appointment with Dave was about to start.

Permission to Dream

Dave was smiling, relaxed, and inviting. He led them into the main lobby of the Carlton Hotel. It was luxurious and quiet, the perfect place for a deep coaching conversation. There were majestic carpets in the long hallways of the hotel with large conference rooms on both sides. A fire was roaring in the gigantic fireplace, and there were several meeting areas centrally located near the fire. They sat in a quiet corner on some brown leather chairs situated between some beautiful potted trees.

"So, Nolan," Dave began, "tell me a little bit about yourself."

They sat for an hour in the warmth of the meeting space while Nolan poured out his entire life story to Dave. Dave sat quietly and listened, asking questions as they went along.

Nolan felt something open up in his heart as he shared. He needed this. There just weren't people out there who took the time to listen to him. As Nolan finished up telling his story, Dave was kind. "Man, you have been through a lot! I can't imagine how difficult it has been to remain hopeful."

Nolan confessed, "Yes, life has had its share of ups and downs for sure. I'm hopeful because for the first time in my life, it feels like I've got something with this real estate business that could turn the tide for me and my family.

The 7 Spheres of a FriendMaker

I really believe things can be different!"

"Nolan, thank you for being vulnerable with me. Can I ask you a question?"

"Of course!" Nolan responded.

"What is it that you want in life?"

Nolan had been counting on this question. He opened up the notebook he had bought and written in earlier.

As he read his desires for his life out loud, he shared what he had felt earlier with Dave, "I feel like I've got Permission to dream again." Dave sat silently and listened until Nolan finished. Then he looked Nolan squarely in the eyes and asked him, "Would you like me to help you with that?"

Nolan reacted, "Ha, well, I don't know how you can, but sure. I'm game."

Warm Fires

Dave directed Nolan's attention to the huge fireplace. They could feel the warmth of the fire on their skin as they talked. "You feel that fire, Nolan?"

Nolan laughed. "Yeah, man, it's pretty awesome. In fact, this whole place is pretty cool. I've never been in here!"

Dave smiled. "This place is my meeting spot for a lot of my one-on-ones. There's a reason why. You see, this fire represents more than just a great place to have a fireside chat. It represents your life."

Nolan looked a little confused. "Ok, go on."

"Nolan, what I'm about to give you has changed my life and the way I do business. Some people might look at my

Warm Fires

way of going about business and think, "That guy's crazy". But what I'm going to tell you is what the poet Robert Frost described as 'the road less traveled.' It's not less traveled because it's hard; it's less traveled because sometimes it's messy and often times it makes you more vulnerable. It's less traveled because it's not as popular as the road most salespeople travel. It's less traveled because it is riskier. But it's worth it, and you'll soon learn why.

"As I was saying before, your life is like this fire. Like this fire, the energy that you release can be warm and inviting. People stop by this fire all day long, especially when it gets cold outside to warm their hands by it. Imagine if your life was a warm fire for people to come and warm their hands by? Imagine if you were the kind of businessperson whose presence was magnetic like a warm fire? Imagine if you could learn how to become that kind of person by changing a few things about the way you do life? Imagine if, by spending some time with me, warming yourself by my fire, I could teach you how to dwell in the spaces of life where this kind of life can be cultivated? It is here, next to my 'fire' that I can teach you about a way of doing business that will yield you the kind of work and life that you really want. I call this way of doing business 'FriendMaking.'"

Nolan was interested, but FriendMaking? *This is his strategy? What is this? Sesame Street?*, he scoffed internally. He had his reservations. Who would possibly build their entire business around friendships? Isn't that a foolish way to try and make a living. Relationships are a necessity, but friendship? *People aren't that trustworthy*, Nolan thought. *They aren't worth risking that kind of connection with, are they?*

Dave read his thoughts. "You think this is too simple, don't you? I can see it in your eyes, Nolan. I understand, but I want you to hang in here with me. Think of your life and business as a series of spheres in which you live and move and exist.

The 7 Spheres of a FriendMaker

We often use the phrase 'sphere of influence' to describe that group of people that dwells within arm's reach of us and that we interact with either through constant communication or occasional conversation. In marketing terms, we call these people your 'warm market.' Isn't it crazy how in business we turn relationships into a cold commodity? I don't like to commoditize my relationships. I prefer to just use the term 'friends.' The people in your sphere of influence know, like, and trust you. These people are probably in the contact list of your phone. If you were to call them today, they would likely pick the phone up or at least call or text you back if you reached out to them. Why do you think that is, Nolan?" Dave asked knowingly.

Nolan didn't have to think long, "Well...because, for the most part, these are my friends."

"Exactly, Nolan. They are your friends. And how did you become friends with them?" Dave's eyes lit up.

"Well, at one point or another along the way, we met and we enjoyed each other's company or we were useful to each other, so I got their contact information and we began hanging out or stayed in touch with one another." Nolan began to nod his head in understanding.

"Nolan, you're on the right track. I want to take you back to ancient times for a moment. The Greek philosopher Aristotle had some interesting insight on friendship. He said that there are actually three levels of friendship: Friendships of utility, friendships of pleasure, and friendships of the good.[13] The first two kinds of friendship (utility and pleasure) are more of an accidental kind of friendship. These kinds of friendships are meaningful for the moment, but definitely temporary and typically lack a real relational depth. The last kind of friendships, friendships of the good, are more intentional and relational. These are the kinds of friendships that last and that are built on mutual appreciation of one another. These types of friendships are relationships built, not on usefulness or emotional fulfillment, but on something else entirely."

He went on, "Friendships of utility are friendships that are there for your benefit. Maybe they are friends who have a skill or gift that benefits you when they are around. These are friends who are useful to you.

"Friendships of pleasure are also friendships that are there for your benefit because it brings you great joy to be around these people. They may not be practically useful relationships, but they are friendships of pleasure.

"Friendships of the good are friendships that have a higher place on the list. We will talk more about these kinds of relationships later. Suffice it to say that motive is everything! And when you can begin to be in relationship with people not for what they bring you, but for what you bring to them, you will gain more from life and business than you ever thought possible.

"I know. It sounds counterintuitive, but it's true. When you are in relationships of the good, your life begins to bear more fruit, not less."

Nolan shrank a little bit in his seat. All of this was interesting, but it also made him extremely nervous.

"You're thinking about the risk involved aren't you, Nolan?" Dave read his mind.

"Yes. It just seems too risky! What if things go south in a business deal? Isn't that just asking for trouble? Why be that vulnerable with people? Won't they use your relationship against you?"

Dave nodded, "Yes." His answer was curt.

Nolan was confused. "Why would I risk so much if I want

to build a business? Aren't I supposed to be thinking about profitability? Isn't there a better way?"

Dave looked at Nolan with compassion. "I understand your fear, Nolan. And truthfully, I have learned the hard way in my life that there are many people in this world who really don't care that much about anything but themselves and their money. Lots of folks have become profitable by keeping an arm's distance from people and keeping everything strictly business. But I've come to understand that anything that is worthwhile in life is worth taking risks for, because the goal of business isn't really about money. It's about something greater."

These words opened up wounds inside of Nolan's spirit. He had known the sting of broken relationships, both personally and professionally. He had felt the pain of having people he knew and trusted betraying that trust. He had spent most of the last ten years of his life insulating himself and his family from this kind of vulnerability because of the pain those kinds of relationships had caused him and his wife. The thought of putting himself and his family in that place of vulnerability again was asking a lot.

"I don't know if I can do this, Dave," Nolan said timidly. "With so much of my family's stability and future riding on this, it just feels like I'm putting us right back into a vulnerable and risky place. And I'm just not sure if I'm willing to do that again. Can't you just give me five tips on how to get more business for myself?"

Dave paused. He looked at Nolan with a true sense of understanding and said, "Nolan, I've been right where you are, and I'm going to tell you something that not many people know. At one point in my life, I had to go through three years of intense counseling to recover from the trauma of past relationships and the scars they left behind in my professional business journey. Taking the hits, walking into the unknown, breaking new ground, pioneering new territories, forging new paths, and developing new relationships all takes time, effort, hard work, and a heck of a lot of risk. I'm not going to tell you that this will be easy. And I certainly don't want to paint a picture for you that makes you think you won't get hurt or that you will be able to avoid being in a vulnerable space. I'm not going to teach you how to become a millionaire in seven easy steps. That's not how this works. What I can tell you is that I'm going to introduce to you a concept that will become the foundation of your life and prop up your business, generate leads for you, and get you in the running for creating a better life for you and your family and a successful business that will bring more satisfaction than any profits you can imagine.

"There are many aspects of running a good business, and I'm not going to get into all the nuts and bolts of marketing, sales, and getting your name and brand out there. This is really more about the foundation of your business and getting started. Do you understand?"

Nolan paused apprehensively. "You know, in all my years of work, I haven't had anyone speak with such clarity and confidence. I appreciate your honesty and vulnerability. I could probably do with some good counseling myself. But I really want to hear what you have to say, so keep going. I'm ready."

Dave began, "Well, first off, Nolan, let me acknowledge something you said. Counseling would do us all a lot of good. There's a lot of stuff that we learned how to do as children to help us cope with the struggles we had when we were younger that we've carried on in life as adults. Some of us really need to do more work than others on getting the soul healing that we need that will release us from our past so we can move unchained into the future.

"With that in mind, I want to talk about your future, not your past. You are a stand-up guy, Nolan. I can tell. But you've got to believe in yourself before you can expect any-

The 7 Spheres of a FriendMaker

one else to believe in you. What I want to lead you into is a process that will change the way you approach everything. I'm not just talking about business, although, for our purposes, that's where I'll spend the bulk of my time. But learning how to get a sense of where your mind, heart, and activity dwells on a daily basis is what this is all about. Learning this stuff will change your life, your home, and your family, not just your business.

"Something new is on the horizon in the business world. When you begin to see that the new economy around us is evolving into something much warmer and more relational than what we have always thought in the past, you understand that the future of business is going to have to move into the realm of authenticity, real-life interaction, consistent presence and proximity to actual people, and learning how to dwell in what I like to call the Seven Spheres of a FriendMaker.

"Your principal goal in business now must shift from *How many clients do I have?* to *How many friends can I make?* And here's the reason: friendship is the foundation of all successful business. And if that is true, which I believe it is, then the mantra of the FriendMaker has to be, 'He who dies with the most friends, wins!'"

Nolan was overwhelmed at this point. He had never heard anyone speak with such confidence about friend-making before. "I never knew there was so much to this."

Dave smiled. "Nolan, this is just the beginning. I want to teach you how to be a FriendMaker. Would you be interested in coming along for the ride?"

"You know, Dave, I think I am. I've tried everything else. Who knows, maybe this is the way?"

Dave nodded. "Listen, Nolan, I'm not talking about a silver bullet here. What I am talking about is a way of life. I'm starting a new eight-session FriendMaker mentoring workshop next Thursday evening at my office. I always do it at the end of the year because this is the time when most of my friends in business start to think about how to make next year really count. Why don't you just look at your schedule and see if you can make it one weekend?"

Nolan already knew his answer. They shook hands and left the hotel.

Nolan's heart was full of hope. "Could this be what I've been hoping for in this business?" he whispered nervously to himself. "What will this do for me and my family that a bunch of lead generating strategy training can't do?"

He was about to find out.

PART THREE:
"The FriendMaker WorkShop"

"Unused truth is lost truth." [14]
Michal Frost & Alan Hirsch

CHAPTER 5
Learning to Ask for Help

Nolan knew he'd been sold. From the time he met Fran in the coffee shop right up until he met Dave, Nolan was convinced that this was what he had been missing. Dave Sawyer's FriendMaker workshop was just around the corner, and he couldn't wait to learn some new strategies for turning his business around.

Dave's FriendMaker workshop was not like anything Nolan had ever been to before. The two-day seminar was much more intimate. There were nine people in the group, and Dave was the leader. Nolan didn't know any of the other eight, but he was eager to get to know them all. They were all businesspeople, each with differing levels of financial success, but they were all in the first five years of owning their business, and none of them felt they had created a sustainable level of business to trust a lifetime to.

The meeting began in Dave's oasis of an office. A small turn-of-the-century stone-built cottage just off the town square, the office was very similar to the hotel where Dave

The 7 Spheres of a FriendMaker

and Nolan had met. The large conference room had a comfortable feel. There was a fireplace, and there were some couches placed in a circle. The dark browns and tans in the room gave it warmth. Each arm of the couch had a small tray attached to it so everyone could take notes while Dave spoke. The atmosphere felt more like a living room session than any seminar Nolan had ever been to.

Dave began the meeting by giving everyone a small piece of paper with a simple phrase written on it. As Nolan opened it up, he knew it accurately described his current mentality. The paper only had four words written in bold ink: *I NEED YOUR HELP*.

Dave began, "Friends, I want you to embed these four words deeply in your mind because over the next two days, you are going to be speaking these words to everyone in this room. Everybody in this workshop is going to know by the end of the next forty-eight hours that you are incapable of building your business or doing your life without them."

"When we break for each session, I want you to say these words every time your meet someone new. Begin every introduction with, "Hello, my name is _____, and *I need your help!*" Everyone looked at each other and smiled uncomfortably.

"I want you to understand something very basic about the journey upon which we are about to embark," Dave continued. "You need people to succeed in business. You need people to make it through life. I want you to hold onto these words and put them somewhere that you can see them every day as you begin your day. Put them on the mirror in your bathroom, stick them to the alarm clock you see every morning, or tattoo them on your wrist so you can look down every day and remind yourself of this truth: I NEED YOUR HELP.

Learning to Ask for Help

"You see, folks, you are not going to be able to do what you want to do these next 48 hours without asking for help. There are no self-made people. Even the best of us don't become the best without the help of others."

Nolan felt like this was extreme. It made him feel too exposed. Dave asked everyone to talk about what they felt when he gave them the little slip of paper, and Nolan could tell that some of the folks there were really nervous about this whole thing just like him.

Dave said, "Humility is the first lesson of the Friend-Maker. If you cannot admit your need for help, you cannot be the help that your community needs. If friendship is the foundation of your business, humility is be the foundation of friendship. You cannot be friends with people you are not humbly serving in some way. I'm sure you've heard this before, but business is about service. Success is not about making money or climbing a ladder. Success is about who you are becoming in the process of building what you are building. As Earl Nightingale says, it is the "progressive realization of a worthy goal." It is a worthy goal to become something greater, better, stronger, and more relational every day.

Here's another thought for you: Money is a by-product of friendship and excellent service. Let me say that again. *Money is a by-product of friendship and excellent service!* We are reaching for more than just dollars and cents here. I am trying to achieve a more holistic approach to business that doesn't cheat people out of their greatest asset in the business transaction, which is you. You are the greatest resource you have. You are also the greatest asset your client has.

"People are the reason we do what we do right now. People will continue to be the reason we do what we do. Once you realize that this business is about chasing people and not transactions, you'll be well on your way to seeing profits in your business and growth in your life.

The 7 Spheres of a FriendMaker

"The principles I'm going to teach you in this eight-part series are about making friends, keeping them, and building a business where your friends use you, refer you, and recommend you to the people they do business within your city. There is nothing new in these truths, but, as the saying goes, unused truth is lost truth.[15] And so, let us dive together into these important spheres and see if we can unearth some of these lost truths.

Nolan and the other folks in the group looked around at each other. They liked everything that Dave was saying. He was inspiring, practical, and incredibly selfless as he shared his vision for being and training up FriendMakers in business.

"Hey everybody, let's take a break. I'll give you a few minutes then we will begin the session on friendship as the foundation of every business. I'll see you back here in five!"

The Foundation of All Good Business

Nolan headed to the coffee machine in the corner of the office. Treats were laid out for everyone to indulge in during the evening session. As he met and mingled with the other business owners that were there, Nolan realized he could be friends with these folks! He thought, I mean, not just for networking purposes which help me, but we could really help one another to make an impact in our town together!

Dave came over and chatted with everyone. Nolan could tell he had taken his time getting to know each person in the room prior to the meeting. He asked people about their families and their personal lives. Smiling, joking, and really enjoying people seemed to be Dave's mode of operation. The other businesspeople in the room were solid folks. There was a baker, a banker, a restaurant owner, a small retail store owner, another real estate agent, a mortgage broker, an insurance agent, a financial advisor and Nolan. Nolan felt comfortable around everyone except the other agent. He just felt weird being around his competition at a seminar like this.

Dave called everyone back into the circle of couches and resumed the session. "Ok everybody, I've given you another piece of paper to write your thoughts on. I'm going to make a statement, and I want you take five minutes to write down what thoughts come to mind when you hear it. Be brutally honest if necessary. Ready? Here we go. 'Friendship is the foundation of everything.' Write down your thoughts and then we can really talk about why we are here tonight."

Everyone got busy writing. Dave played some Christmas music on a small radio above the fireplace mantle. This got most everyone's creative juices flowing except a few people Dave noticed struggling to come up with something to write.

"I want honesty more than anything else," Dave insisted. "I don't necessarily want you to agree with me. Give me some pushback. What objections do you have regarding this approach?"

Nolan really gave it some thought. It seemed silly, mixing business and friendship. It was socially taboo. Why would Dave push this idea? Nolan hadn't come here to make friends. He, like the others, was there to learn how to make money, establish himself in the business world, and climb to the top. He didn't have time for relationships, much less friendships.

Dave laughed. "I see you guys scoffing at me! You're telling me with your body language that it can't be done. No, that you won't be doing this. I can feel your energy, guys, and I get it. It doesn't seem like anyone values friendship anymore. But I think we need a primer on friendship first to set the expectations of our time together."

The 7 Spheres of a FriendMaker

Aristotle's Three Levels of Friendship

"I'll start with Aristotle's three levels of friendship, and then I'll give you my twist on how this relates to business. Then we will talk about the seven spheres of friendship and what you will gain by dwelling in them.

"From our first conversation, when I introduced the concept of FriendMaker to each of you, we spoke about the three levels of friendship: friendships of utility, pleasure, and the good. I want to show you how each of these levels is necessary and can lead to what I will call the best kind of friendships.

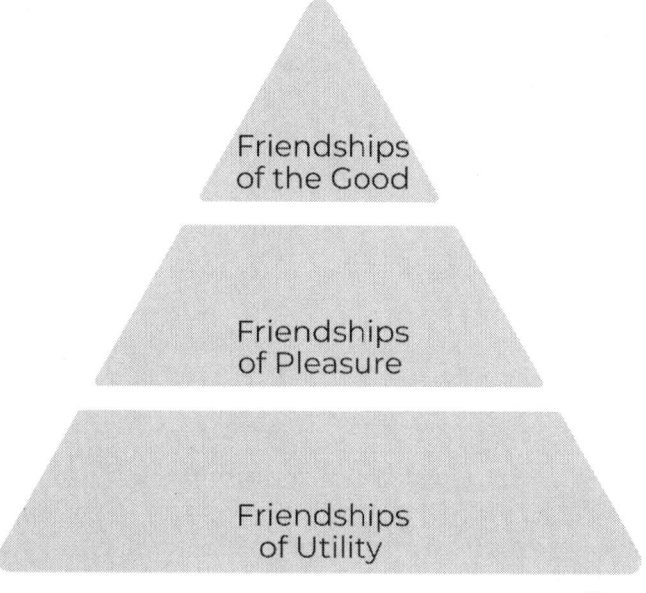

Friendships of the Good

Friendships of Pleasure

Friendships of Utility

Aristotle's 3 Levels of Friendship[13]

"The first level of relating to people usually comes to us as a friendship of utility. We often meet people based on our needs. Not only do we need people, but they need us. We have relationships that exist for the sole purpose of having our personal needs met. Now, I'm not going to put a moral compass on this idea. It's true, but that doesn't make it a right or wrong kind of thing. This is simply a fact.

Learning to Ask for Help

We use people. They use us. We have needs, they have needs. Relationships are good for us because they are useful to us. But this isn't the only value of friendship. It is the base level, the entry level of friendship. We often begin relationships with people simply because they meet our basic needs.

"The second level of relating to people comes through our need for enjoyment and pleasure. We pursue these relationships because we have a need to enjoy life. Life is hard and difficult at times. Suffering happens. There are social difficulties, political difficulties, financial difficulties, relational difficulties... the list is long and goes on and on. Life is hard. It makes sense that we need to experience pleasure. We enter friendships of pleasure for the simple fact that we need to laugh, to enjoy life, and to feel good. The deeper we go into friendship with people, the closer we become. And when we get closer to people, we get to express our needs and they do the same with us. These relationships of pleasure often turn into the strongest and most intimate relationships we have as we get vulnerable with people and grow in friendship.

"Finally, the third level of friendships are friendships of the good. These are relationships that have been built on the foundation of our need for the usefulness of people and the pleasure of their company. But relationships of the good form as we realize that selfish fulfillment of our own needs is not the highest value in friendship. We don't simply need people for what they can do for us and how they can make us feel. We need people because they need us. We understand that relationship in itself is a healing catalyst for something much more impactful in this world than selfish ambition.

"Asking people for help is awkward. Telling them that you need help can seem very self-serving. That's why it is important that you bring more value to others than you ask them to bring to you. If you've been spending your life

The 7 Spheres of a FriendMaker

only asking for help from others but never giving anything away, then it's going to be super awkward. But if you position yourself in the lives of the people around you where you bring more value than what you are asking from them, then it is only natural for people to want to help you.

"You bring value to your friends and they bring value to you, but the motive is different. You aren't in relationships of the good for what they do for you but rather for what you do for them. Generosity, service, giving, and loving are all valuable assets in relationships of the good.

"You will reap the benefits of this life when your life becomes all about being the kind of person who values people over profits, friendship over financial success, and relationships over rewards.

"With this foundational understanding of how friendship works and the ways in which it develops in our personal life, I want to submit to you that the way you build a business is very similar to the way you build a life of friendships.

"Foundationally, friendships of utility are the entry point for people who find your business. There is something that your business offers to people that is useful. You have a product or a service that is useful to people and they enter into a relationship with you because they like you. As a by-product of their affinity for you and their need for the product or service you provide, they will usually end up purchasing that product or service from you.

"Now, if you do what most people in business do, you will provide a product or service to people that is useful and then hope that they come back again once that product or service has run out of its usefulness, correct?"

Everyone looked around the room and nodded their heads.

Learning to Ask for Help

"Well," said Dave, "I want to teach you how you can develop these important relational skills by introducing you to the Seven Spheres of a FriendMaker. Let's take a quick break then I'll come back, and we'll get started.

CHAPTER 6
The 7 Spheres of a FriendMaker

The room was buzzing by this time. Nolan had a few brief conversations with some of the other business owners in the room. Everyone was certainly curious about what Dave was talking about. There was still a sense of hesitation in the eyes of everyone he spoke with. Could this truly be the most important part of business? Could this be foundational truth?

Dave called everyone back to the circle, put up a graphic on the screen, and began the next session. Everyone was all ears.

"By now," Dave began, "since you are in business, you have probably already heard about the importance of having a database, a sphere, or a list of contacts. I'm not going to re-invent the wheel here. There are many great resources on how to build a large database. Instead, I want to teach you how to deepen what I like to call 'relational equity' with the people who are on your list of friends. Relational equity is the value of the depth and breadth of

The 7 Spheres of a FriendMaker

your relationships. How many people do you know who have a large base of friends and clients but who aren't very close with any of them? How many people do you know who have a great depth of relationship with their friends and clients, but don't have many contacts? It is more important to go deep with a few than to be shallow with many. But making sure that the number of people you go deep with is enough to create a sustainable stream of referral business in the years to come is also a critical component of good business.

"As I've discussed with all of you in our fireside chats, I want you to think of your life and business as a series of spheres in which you live and move and breathe. In marketing terms, we call these people your 'warm market.' I prefer to use the term 'friends.' I told Nolan the other day that I really don't like to commoditize my relationships. Isn't it crazy how in business we turn relationships into just a cold commodity? What if we stopped looking at our customers as commodities and started realizing we were in the process of building community?"

Light bulb. That was exactly what most of the business owners in the room had experienced. Business seemed to always be a commodity exchange not a community exchange. Dave hit the nail on the head. Nolan's mind began to race.

"Moving on," Dave continued, "More than just sales skills are required to help you understand what I'm getting after. There are many systems and plans out there for you created by qualified professionals and coaching companies to follow for a to-do list of activities that will help you gain success in your business.

"What I'm here to talk to you about today is a supplement to those hard sales skills necessary to growing your business. I want to teach you some ways to become

The 7 Spheres of a FriendMaker

the kind of person people will want to do business with. This is a different conversation altogether because it challenges you at your core, your spirit. It is in your heart and your spirit where your mind can be made up to become the kind of person you need to be before you walk into the activities that help you build the business you want to build. This is what the Seven Spheres of FriendMaking are all about!"

A Critical Understanding of Where We are Going

Dave rummaged through his bag and pulled out a fresh pineapple and set it on the podium at the front for all eyes to see. Dave collected his thoughts and began to share, "What is this?"

"A Pineapple!!" someone shouted from the back. "Exactly," Dave grinned. "And what do you think of when you see this symbol out there in the world?" People started shouting out words, "Vacation!" "Sweetness" "Tropical Paradise!" The crowd started to mumble something under their breath. Dave noticed there was some hesitation. "Say it out loud friends. Don't be shy!"

Nolan volunteered to represent the mumblers. He was trying hard not to laugh. "They're saying that it represents something that might not be appropriate in this setting." Dave beckoned it out of him, "C'mon Nolan, what did they say?"

"Swingers, Dave," Nolan said sheepishly, "The pineapple represents swingers." The crowd busted out laughing. Dave laughed too.

"Well, that is not the message I'm trying to convey," Dave chuckled. "So let's see if we can redeem this symbol in our workshop today!" After the laughter died down some, Dave began again, "There is a reason I have chosen to use a pineapple as the symbol for the FriendMaker.

The 7 Spheres of a FriendMaker

You see the seven spheres graphic is topped with a pineapple crown because I wanted to tie this idea of being a FriendMaker to a symbol that has for generations been a picture of friendship. I've brought this pineapple out as an object lesson and a reminder throughout our time together of this very important symbol of hospitality and friendship.

"The pineapple was discovered shortly after Christopher Columbus made his landing in the Caribbean islands. He took it back to Europe where it soon became a delicacy and topped the tables of the wealthiest in society. Pretty soon, because of its popularity at social events and feasts, it took on a symbolic meaning of friendship and hospitality. Upon arrival at a party or when invited to a home for a social engagement, it was not unusual to bring a pineapple with you as a symbol of friendship.

"Pineapples became such a symbol of warmth and friendship for families in the new world that they would carve images of pineapples into the lentils and doorposts of their homes. This imagery is perfect for you in understanding the message of the FriendMaker. Like the warm fire that burns in this fireplace and the pineapple that symbolizes friendship among strangers, I want you to become so warm and inviting to your clients that they will want to do business with you not just one time, but repeatedly into the future.

Your Circle versus Your Sphere

Dave kept challenging everyone's thinking. "Another symbol I have chosen to use in my FriendMaking business philosophy is that of a sphere." Dave pointed everyone's attention to the screen on the wall. On it, there was a picture of two circles. On one side there was a two-dimensional line-drawn circle. On the other side was a three-dimensional sphere.

The 7 Spheres of a FriendMaker

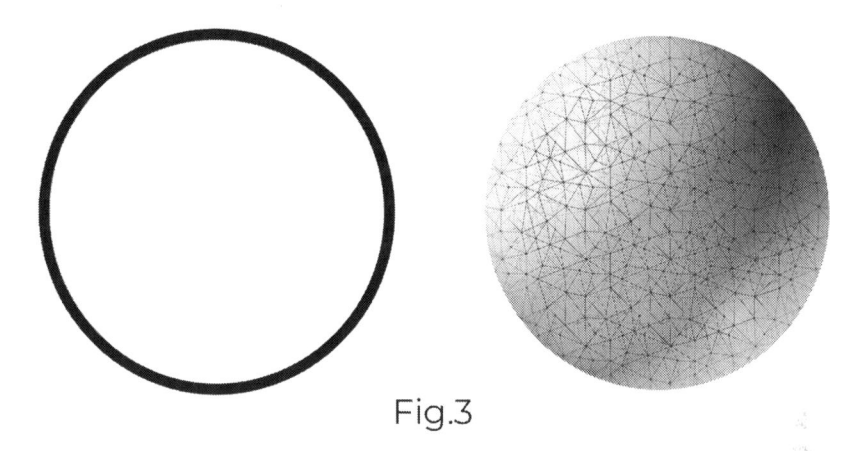

Fig.3

"Look at figure 3," Dave instructed. "When you look at a circle, what do you see? Is it two dimensional or three dimensional? Is it a simple shape or does it have some complexity to it? What about a sphere? What do you see?"

Some feedback from the audience came. "I see simplicity versus complexity." "I see depth and no depth." Dave reciprocated their thoughts.

"Exactly," he quipped. "Circles are two-dimensional. They are flat and have no depth. Circles are easy. They are easy to draw, and they are easy to understand. Your circle of friends might be a mile wide and an inch deep. I like to think of social media friends as that two-dimensional circle of relationships. Most of these people are just connection points, not people you have an actual relationship with.

"A sphere, however, is three-dimensional and more complex. It has depth and volume. In a 3-D sphere of friends there is a sense that you have room to explore more of what's inside. There is a mystery to it. What is inside of there? How can I learn more about that sphere?

"The reason that I have chosen to teach you these Seven

The 7 Spheres of a FriendMaker

Spheres of FriendMaking is that I want to teach you how to step into the mystery and depth of each area of your clients' lives, hearts, and minds. What I want to teach you is not simply some two-dimensional skills you need to develop, but three-dimensional spheres in which you need to learn how to *dwell*."

Two Things

"As we journey into the seven spheres, we are going to discuss two important ideas that you need to develop within each sphere:
1. New Attitudes.
2. New Practices.

"In this training, I will teach you how to develop the general attitude of each sphere and then describe for you practices that will help you embody that attitude with the people in your business and life. My goal for you in this training is that by the time you are finished with this workshop, you will be able to build a business of friends. The way you achieve this goal is by dwelling in the seven spheres of a FriendMaker."

Creating a Different Experience

"Have you ever done business with someone who you felt was shady? Have you ever had a bad experience with a business or individual? How did that make you feel about working with them in the future? What kind of impression did it leave you with regarding the industry they were in?

"You see, too many people have had negative experiences with sales/business people in our world. And as a result, they are not optimistic about what they are going to experience when they work with you. For others, their opinion of you and your respective industry has been tainted. For example, realtors who don't approach their business professionally and treat their clients respectfully, often end up making those clients leave their real estate transaction with a bad taste in their mouths. When given the opportunity a second time to use a realtor for a real estate transaction, those clients will likely look for alternative ways to make a transaction happen where it doesn't involve an agent.

"This causes a significant problem in the market because now many buyers and sellers are skeptical of shady salespeople taking advantage of them. They are reluctant to step into an environment with an agent if they haven't experienced a warm, inviting, and safe space to walk through a transaction.

"The natural result for the average consumer is to look for a way of doing business that doesn't require them to have to deal with too many people. People are untrustworthy, unkind, and unconcerned about their clients' well-being. It's safer and easier to deal with someone in an impersonal way so that we don't have to go through the pain of dealing with people who don't really care about us. And guess who has cashed in on this mistrust that has happened to the average consumer?" Dave paused.

"Big Box companies!" came the answer from the back of the room. Another voice came swiftly from the side, "Corporate America!"

"That's right!" Dave quipped.

"And at what cost to the consumer does this all come? I am convinced that consumers are missing out on several things. When a customer chooses the route of an impersonal business transaction, they are missing some very elemental human needs. Namely, that of a personal guide to:

The 7 Spheres of a FriendMaker

- Reassure them they are doing the right thing.
- Give them confidence in their decision making.
- Educate them in their knowledge of what they are dealing with.
- Navigate them through the uncharted territory.

"That's when I identified the seven spheres. I have organized these spheres into a systematic and specific progression that, if you will follow it, will help you to guide your client into a more personal sales experience than they've ever had before.

"The seven spheres are going to help you understand the needs of your clients and how to create the kind of environment where your client will experience the meeting of these needs in a warm, relational way. You will create a different experience for the people who interact with your business. In return, you will generate new leads for your business through strong referrals. You will also create a warm fire of your business that will be a safe and inviting space for people to come in proximity with. The reason you want to do this is so that when people need the service or product you provide, they will trust you to be their vendor of choice when it comes to purchasing that service or product again in the future.

"The Seven Spheres are as follows:

1. The Sphere of Listening
2. The Sphere of Learning
3. The Sphere of Liking
4. The Sphere of Loyalty
5. The Sphere of Leaping
6. The Sphere of Leading
7. The Sphere of Loving
   (See Fig. 4)

"Tomorrow let's unpack these seven spheres together. But be prepared to be challenged. This is about becoming a better person so you can serve your clients better. As you

The 7 Spheres of a FriendMaker

dwell in these spheres, you will change. And so will the lives of the people you serve." And with that, Dave pulled out a knife, cut the pineapple, and asked, "Now, anybody want a slice?"

the 7 spheres of a FriendMaker

1

Sphere #1: The Sphere of Listening
A FriendMaker *Listens* to their clients
By listening to their clients, sales people communicate an attitude of *Attentiveness.*

2

Sphere #2: The Sphere of Learning
A FriendMaker *Learns* their clients
By learning their clients, sales people communicate an attitude of *Understanding.*

3

Sphere #3: The Sphere of Liking
A FriendMaker *Likes* their clients
By liking their clients, sales people communicate an attitude of *Respect.*

④

Sphere #4: The Sphere of Loyalty
A FriendMaker is *Loyal* to their clients
By showing loyalty to their clients, sales people communicate *Advocacy*.

⑤

Sphere #5: The Sphere of Leaping
A FriendMaker *Leaps* for their clients
By leaping for their clients, sales people communicate an attitude of *Risk-Taking*.

⑥

Sphere #6: The Sphere of Leading
A FriendMaker *Leads* their clients
By leading their clients, sales people communicate an attitude of high quality *Service*.

⑦

Sphere #7: The Sphere of Loving
A FriendMaker *Loves* their clients
By loving their clients well, long after they sell them a product of service, sales people communicate an attitude of authentic *Care*.

Fig. 4

Author's Note

As we move into the main content of this workshop, I have split up each of the chapters into two parts: "Workshop Session" and "Workshop Notes". The Workshop Session is that of Dave Sawyer interacting with the workshop group. This is to keep the continuity of the story and to help the flow.

The Workshop Notes are the actual core content of the workshop. These notes describe two things:

1. The attitude that the sphere is trying to convey.
2. The practices that you can put into place to develop that attitude.

This is where the non-fiction principles meet the fictional characters in the book. I have interjected my own experiences and lessons learned into the Workshop Notes. I hope by doing it this way, you can still get some of the story mixed in with the practical side of the content.

The 7 Spheres of a FriendMaker

As business coach Brian Buffini says, "Education without implementation is merely entertainment."[16] It is my hope that this material will help you be able to think through ways you can implement these attitudes and practices into your own business.

WORKSHOP SESSION #1
LISTEN TO YOUR CLIENT

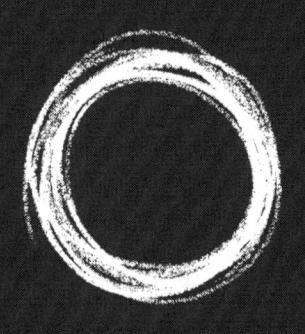

Chapter 7
The Sphere of Listening:
The Attitude of Attentiveness

The next morning, the workshop continued. Dave then invited everyone over to the fire and had everyone pull their chairs in close.

"My mother used to tell me that God gave us two ears and one mouth so that we could listen twice as much as we speak. Have you ever heard this? And yet, how many of us, when we first engage with a new person regarding our product or service end up vomiting information all over them from the get-go?

"I want to encourage you to resist the temptation to be the person speaking the most when you first begin working with a client. Your client doesn't want you to be the hero in their story. They want to be the hero. They want to be the ones deciding whether they want to work with you, but they won't feel that the opportunity is being given to them if the only person speaking in a sales conversation is you."

The 7 Spheres of a FriendMaker

Nolan stopped to think as Dave was speaking. He knew what Dave was saying was true. Nolan liked to talk. He liked to speak and be heard by people all the time. The Sphere of Listening had always been a difficult one to dwell in for him.

Dave continued, "I know that you know more than your client about the product or service you are providing them, but the time for speaking about your vast knowledge is not at the beginning of the conversation. That opportunity will present itself. You must begin your conversation by asking questions and listening to your client.

"It's another cliche, but people really don't care how much you know until they know how much you care. Caring and compassion are not common traits in the business world. Have you ever heard, 'It's a dog-eat-dog world out there'? Or 'Might is right' and 'Survival of the fittest'? These methods of engaging with people will not endear you to them. They will most likely repel them.

"Listen to your clients. Begin by asking them how you can help them. Ask them what brought them to your storefront or what made them call you. Ask them about their families, their work, their fun, and their passion. (aka. The F.O.R.D Method) Listen to their answers and figure out where their pain is.

"Every potential client or customer has a problem that needs solving. You won't know what it is if you don't listen to them. And they won't speak it out to you unless you ask them. Don't be afraid to ask probing questions. And don't be ashamed of asking questions that make them think or that challenge their assumptions about what you provide."

This was all good stuff. Nolan was writing down every word. He thought about all the times he had engaged with people who had come to him asking questions about real estate. He knew a lot and was happy to give out information that would be helpful to people. But he was

The Sphere of Listening: The Attitude of Attentiveness

also guilty of giving people information that they didn't ask for.

"Listening is a skill to develop as well as a sphere to dwell in," Dave proceeded. "When you create an atmosphere of listening around you, you give people the opportunity to be heard. And when people feel heard, they respond in kind. They want you to help them solve their problems. And listening opens the door to seeing the problems your clients are struggling with."

LISTENING

WORKSHOP NOTES

THE SPHERE OF LISTENING

The goal of a FriendMaker in the Sphere of Listening is *attentiveness*. As Dave Sawyer tells Nolan in the seminar, "You want to give people the opportunity to be heard. When people feel heard, they respond in kind." The way we become better listeners is by practice. Does practice make perfect? Honestly, that doesn't matter. What practice really does is it trains you to really attend to people's needs so they will want to do business with you.

The 7 Spheres of a FriendMaker

Attentiveness in the Sphere of Listening for a FriendMaker shows up in three intentional practices.

1. Shut off distractions.
2. Ask lots of questions.
3. Take plenty of notes.

PRACTICE #1 - SHUT OFF DISTRACTIONS.

Clients need to know they have your full attention. Cell phones, computers, and other digital devices, while they can be helpful for many reasons, all serve as 'weapons of mass distraction' for most of us when we are dealing with our clients. If you are meeting with a client, set aside or even turn off your digital devices.

Being distracted when working with your clients communicates to them that you have better things to do rather than spend your time with them. There are countless stories of people who have been turned off by distracted salespeople on their phones in the middle of important conversations.

Put your phone away. Don't just put it face down on the table in front of you. Put it out of sight. Wear a watch so you can keep an eye on the time if you are in a meeting, but give people your fully devoted attention.

Be Present. When you are speaking with someone, engage with them in conversation. Look them in the eyes and resist the temptation to look away when they are speaking to you or when you are speaking with them. Practice good eye contact. Don't let your mind wander. Be disciplined in your thoughts. Give them your full attention in the here and now.

Repeat what you've heard. Repeat back to your clients the things they say to you. Say something like, "So what I'm hearing you say is..." This lets people know that you are really paying attention and listening to them.

The Sphere of Listening: The Attitude of Attentiveness

Active listening, as we discussed before, is a skill that you must develop. It may be the most important skill and the most difficult one to master all at the same time. But you must master it. And the way you do it is by shutting off the distractions both external and internal that seek to hijack a positive interaction with another human being.

PRACTICE #2 - ASK LOTS OF QUESTIONS.

In the seminar, Dave mentions one of the most popular information-gathering techniques for sales-people called the F.O.R.D. method which stands for Family, Occupation, Recreation, & Dreams. As we gather information about people, these four areas are incredibly helpful because "The F.O.R.D. questions represent people's core values...When you ask about these four areas, you are touching their life and making an immediate personal connection."[17]

The best way to engage your clients, your new prospects, and anyone you are meeting for the first time to get to know them better is to ask questions surrounding these four aspects of human life. Everyone has a family of some sort. Ask them if they are married, if they have children, where their family is from. Everyone works. Find out about it by asking what they do for a living, what they do in their job, and how long they've been doing it. Ask about what they like to do for fun. What do they do with their free time? Do they share recreation time with anyone else or do they prefer to be alone? What are they dreaming about? What gets them excited and passionate about life? Take a genuine interest in finding out more about the person so that you can find common ground with them. Once you find common ground, then you have a frame of reference from which to engage more in conversation with them.

Imagine your questions as uncovering treasure that you can share with the person you are speaking with. Listen to their answers. Engage with them personally, not simply professionally.

The 7 Spheres of a FriendMaker

You will sometimes find that people resist answering your questions. Be sure to be sensitive to their demeanor as you ask questions. You are not prying; you are genuinely wanting to get to know them. As you listen to them tell of their lives, their hopes, their families, etc., you will discover what really makes them come alive. You will also be able to learn how you can serve them in their life.

Whatever it is that you do in your business is best done in the context of serving people. As you serve people, you get to know them. As you get to know them, you become a trusted source of the service you provide. This eventually results in people not only trusting you with their personal business, but also their friends, family, co-workers, and neighbors.

Building relationships is how you build your business. And it all begins with learning how to dwell within the Sphere of Listening.

PRACTICE #3 - TAKE PLENTY OF NOTES.

Something I have found that is very helpful in my life and business is to always have a small notepad close by at all times. As I meet people and engage them in conversation, I hear them say things that I believe to be helpful. Writing down what you hear is a way of retaining helpful knowledge, and it is also another way of showing people that you value what it is that they are saying.

Imagine you are sitting down with a client for the first time, and they begin to share with you all of the things they are looking for in a home that they want you to help them find. *Write it down.* Write down everything that would be considered important by this person in their search and let them see you do it. You want to endear yourself to the people you seek to serve. Nothing communicates your care and concern for people more than valuing their time and listening to them. Go back after your conversation is over and review your notes. Take

The Sphere of Listening: The Attitude of Attentiveness

time to remember what it was you and your client were talking about by reading through the notes and ideas you wrote down while it is still fresh in your mind. You'll find that you retain your memory of the conversation better if you go back and review it.

Increase Your Attentiveness

After your conversation is over, maybe ten or fifteen minutes after you leave each other, give the person you just met with a quick phone call to thank them for their time and to communicate appreciation for their trust in you to help them through the process of whatever it is you spoke with them about.

Again, all of this is a means to an end: friendship. You are more likely to enjoy your life and your business more if you focus on creating healthy vibrant relationships with the people you serve than if you don't. People know when you are using them as a commodity to obtain something you want. They also know when you are being genuine and authentic with them. This is not something that can be faked. Remember, your goal isn't using people as commodities to get what you want. Your goal is developing community to help them get what they want.

Some people will use this information so that they can try and manipulate people to help them get what they want. To those people, I would say, "Your sins will find you out." Living a life of manipulation and using human beings is not a sustainable way to make a living, and it will not take you where you really want to end up.

The most successful people I know are people who have seen the power of developing healthy friendships with their clientele and business partners and who have partnered with these people to encourage one another and build families and businesses that will last.

The 7 Spheres of a FriendMaker

It all begins in the Sphere of Listening.

There is a natural progression as each sphere is introduced. Each sphere builds upon the lessons of the one before it. As we move out of the Sphere of Listening, a door is opened to the second sphere, the Sphere of Learning.

WORKSHOP SESSION #2
LEARN YOUR CLIENT

Chapter 8
The Sphere of Learning:
The Attitude of Understanding

Dave spoke with authority as he introduced the second sphere. "This sphere is about learning your clients. But before I talk about learning the people you serve, I think it is important to take a moment and talk about learning your self.

"If you are the kind of person who has the attitude 'I have arrived', then you have a problem with arrogance. You may have a lot of knowledge and skill about your area of expertise in business, but once you think that you have arrived you are in a dangerous place. People who are so disconnected from the real world that they aren't aware of their need for personal growth have lost touch with something that is vital for anyone in the business world: a sense of humility. A dedication to learning through reading, listening to wise and knowledgeable experts, and going to seminars and workshops will result in you growing as a businessperson and a leader. Because so much of what we do as businesspeople is also tied into leadership, the level of your personal growth will directly

The 7 Spheres of a FriendMaker

affect your ability to help lead others you hope to serve in your business.

"If you don't keep growing personally, you won't grow your business professionally. Successful businesspeople are dynamic. They are active in their business and in their pursuit of wisdom. They are dedicated to bettering themselves so they can be more of a benefit to their clients. Choosing not to grow or outright refusing to submit yourself to continual learning will eventually be the death of your business.

Learn Your Clients

"Prowess is defined as 'skill or experience in a particular activity or field.' [18] If you are paying attention to the client in front of you, you will begin to learn more about them. This is as much a skill to develop as a sphere to dwell in. You will learn what makes them tick. You will learn what kind of personality you are dealing with.

"We don't have time to go into all the different personality types here, but one of the most eye-opening journeys I ever made was learning my own personality type. And there are many different ways to learn about yourself. The Myer's Briggs personality test, the 5 Voices Assessment, the DISC Profile, the Enneagram... these are all great and unique ways to understand people. I encourage you to look into all these ways of learning personalities. Not only will you discover how you are wired, but you will also discover how to recognize the kinds of people you are dealing with on a daily basis and how best to learn their communication style so you can better know how to interact with them on a personal basis.

"Learning your clients means studying them, listening to them, letting them tell you their story. I do this with people all the time. 'Will you tell me your story?' is one of my favorite questions to ask. It opens people up in ways you

The Sphere of Learning: The Attitude of Understanding

would never know if you hadn't asked. And it invites learning."

Dave paused for a minute to let these ideas soak into the class. One of the participants asked, "Why is this stuff so important?"

Dave stopped his lecture and began to tell a story. "Jackie was one of my clients when I first got into real estate years ago. She was a quiet and reserved lady who began our business relationship only wanting me to help her find a home. But when we first met, I talked over her head. I told her about what the real estate market was doing, how many clients I had served that year, and I even told her several stories of people who had been in the same situation she was in. She couldn't have cared less. She needed someone to learn her. She didn't care how much gross volume I had done or any of the awards I had won. It did not matter to her what was going on with the local community popularity contest that I had been nominated for.

Then I stopped to listen to her story and I began to learn a little bit more about Jackie. I found out that she was tired and lonely. I also found out that she had been through a recent divorce, lost one of her children in a car wreck a couple of years ago, and that she was currently living in a rented apartment that had a lease that was set to expire in forty-five days. I learned that she was a no-nonsense kind of personality. She just wanted the steps to getting into a home, and she needed me to learn her so I could better understand where she was coming from. Once I stopped long enough to get to know Jackie, I was finally able to help her find what she was looking for and get her into the right home.

"I didn't know how to help her until I stopped talking at her and started listening to her. When I stopped trying to impress her with my accomplishments, my accolades, and my associations, I hit a breakthrough. What she needed

The 7 Spheres of a FriendMaker

was to tell her own story. And so, I listened and learned that she had already been through the process of trying to find a home with three other realtors. They had all done the same thing I had done. Barraged her with information. Spoke at her. Saw her as another potential transaction and nothing else.

"Taking the time to learn your clients does a couple of things. First of all, it lets your client know you see them. People want to be seen, not looked past. They want to be understood and validated, not patronized. Too many times, people feel like they are just another notch on your belt rather than someone with a life and hopes in finding something better. Once I began to learn my clients, I began to see them for who they really were—people who needed to be seen and heard.

"Second of all, it opens up a door for you to serve not only them, but also all the other people in their life that they would be willing to refer business to you. Every person that you encounter is not only a potential sale, but they are also a potential source of future business for you if you treat them right."

LEARNING

The Sphere of Learning: The Attitude of Understanding

WORKSHOP NOTES

THE SPHERE OF LEARNING

The goal of a FriendMaker in the Sphere of Learning is *understanding*. This requires humility and a teachable spirit. As Dave Sawyer tells Nolan in the seminar, "People want to be seen, not looked past." In this sphere, the goal isn't to gain knowledge that we can just spit back out at people. It is to gain understanding of another human being. We want to learn someone else, their personality, their motivations, their dreams, and their needs, wants, and desires.

Stepping into this sphere is stepping into an education of another human being. It is critical that we do this if we are going to become friends with people. We must learn what makes them tick.

Understanding in the Sphere of Learning for a FriendMaker shows up in three intentional practices:

1. Gather information.
2. Find out what they want.
3. Give them room to breathe.

PRACTICE #1: GATHER INFORMATION.

The first thing you must remember when you are working with your client is that they have a history. Everything that you see sitting in front of you in the person you are interacting with is the result of a story that has been going on long before you ever arrived on the scene.

Just like you are the sum of your experiences, so is the person who is there before you. If you are going to gain a proper understanding of your client, you are going to have to ask a lot of questions and gather as much information as you can.

The 7 Spheres of a FriendMaker

You will find that some people are more willing to give you their personal back story than others. Timing is key. Gathering information is an art and a skill. You can't just begin digging too deeply with some people. It is important that you take the time to read their posture, their body language, and their verbal cues.

I don't have to time to go over it in this book, but I will tell you that there is value in understanding the different personality types there are. Mainly because, as you interact with people, you will find that they are all very different. And the main issue for most people is the issue of trust.

People want to trust you. They really do. Many of them have had many bad experiences with untrustworthy salespeople; they will need to warm up to you. Part of understanding people is recognizing their process and the amount of time you may need to invest in helping them adjust to your presence in their life. You want to gather enough information from a person's personal life to be able to find common ground with them and ultimately to serve them better. This will help you really understand what it is that drives and motivates them. This leads us to the next practice.

PRACTICE # 2: FIND OUT WHAT THEY WANT.

The second practice you want to begin doing as you work with your clients and try to gain a better understanding of them is narrowing down the core motivations in their life. The best question to ask your client in the Sphere of Learning is "What do you want?"

Driving down into the depths of what a person wants is so important to understanding them. When you ask this question, what you are really looking for is what is it that makes them come alive. What stirs their affections? What moves them? What is it that they really desire more than anything else?

The Sphere of Learning: The Attitude of Understanding

If you can understand what your clients really want, you can help them to achieve those things. But first you must help them see what it is that they want so you can paint a picture for them of how working with you will help them get just that.

Dwelling in the Sphere of Learning helps you understand your clients and helps your clients see the world differently. When you serve them by learning what it is they want, identifying their core values and motives, then you can help them see the world differently and create hope in them that you can help them achieve their goals.

Rich Litvin, author of The Prosperous Coach, explains, "In my work with coaches, consultants, or even small business owners, I have developed a reputation for doing one thing exceptionally well. My clients create a thriving practice by invitation and referral only. So, although I say I am in the miracle business, what I actually do is help my clients see their world differently. Because when you help someone see their world differently, their world changes. When someone sees the world differently, they show up differently, and they create results that looked impossible a moment before."[19]

Once you've gathered information from your client and identified what they want, it's time to give them some permission to dream with you. I call this 'giving them room to breathe.'

PRACTICE # 3: GIVE THEM ROOM TO BREATHE.

Far too many salespeople smother their clients with information once they get to know them. I've been guilty of it too. You get a new client. You sit down with them to find out who they are and what they want, only to get to the real point of your meeting which is where you smother them with more information than they need in one sitting. What you end up communicating, if you're not careful, is

The 7 Spheres of a FriendMaker

that what you have to say is more important than the story they are telling you.

After your client is overwhelmed with everything you've shared with them, they are now also wondering if you heard anything they said or if you understood anything about them! That little spark of attention that you were giving them that they were hoping was coming from a place of authenticity is quickly doused by their skepticism of you because of how you've turned the conversation away from them and back towards you!

That's why it is so important at this point in the Sphere of Learning that you actually give your client some room to breathe.

Originally, I was going to call this practice "Give Them Room to *Be*." Something it has taken me a long time to realize in my own life is that I must learn to leave room for the awkward silence with people.

I'm an extrovert by nature. The introverts reading this probably already understand that I have no problem with lots of words! But something we all need to remember is that there is power in silence. Silence truly is golden. I believe that is because it is valuable. Silence is so valuable when dealing with our clients because it creates space and margin between us and our clients which is often needed to process our thinking and our conversations. We must give people room to be themselves, to think, and to process.

A phrase I often use when I'm working with my clients is "Trust the process." Sometimes there isn't an immediate solution to a pressing problem. We need to learn that this is ok. Some things just need to work themselves out. And some people need to just have time and space to process the journey we are bringing them through in our business.

The Sphere of Learning: The Attitude of Understanding

We must give our clients room to breathe and room to be.

Increase your Understanding

A client who senses that you are aiming for understanding will count you as trustworthy. As you dwell in the spheres of Listening and Learning, you are building a foundation of trust with your client. When people trust you, they'll let you go to bat for them.

Don't hesitate to call and ask more questions to increase your understanding of your clients. If you don't know something, don't pretend to know something. The "Fake it 'til you make it" mantra that I have heard new salespeople chant when they begin a new business is a pretty lame way to run a business. Honesty is always the best policy. Again, you are trying to build trust. People know when you are lying. If they don't, they'll eventually find out. Build trust with your clients so there is never any question about your integrity throughout the whole process.

I can't express enough how important this is. I am also aware that deeply ingrained habits of untrustworthy behavior may need professional help. Don't think that just because you read a book on how to become friends with people that you don't need to get therapy for issues that are much deeper seated than I can go into here. People need us healthy and at our best so that we can bring the best of ourselves into their process. When we bring people our best, it becomes a much more enjoyable process. And when the process is more enjoyable, we start to move into the Sphere of Liking.

WORKSHOP SESSION #3
LIKE YOUR CLIENTS

Chapter 9
The Sphere of Liking:
The Attitude of Respect

Dave could tell that he had hit a nerve with the folks in the workshop. Everyone was taking notes and responding to him during the Q&A sessions right after each sphere was covered. "As you can tell," Dave summarized, "the first two spheres are foundational to the rest of the spheres. If you don't spend time listening to your clients and learning them, then you short-circuit the process of moving from each sphere to the next.

"Attentiveness and understanding are two attitudes that must permeate your time with your clients. If your clients feel attended to and understood, they will naturally let their guard down with you and allow you to serve them more powerfully.

"This brings me to the third sphere, The Sphere of Liking. Now before I lose you, understand that I'm not talking about people-pleasing here. Dwelling in this sphere is not about trying to make everyone happy with you. There will be moments in your relationship with people that you will

The 7 Spheres of a FriendMaker

have to speak difficult words. There will also be times where you will not like the process or the person in front of you. You can't like everyone. However, what I really am aiming for here is an attitude of respect for your clients.

"No one wants to be endured. No one wants you to simply tolerate them. People want to be listened to, learned, and ultimately, they want you to like them. Just like I know you want your clients to like you, your clients long to be liked as well. They want you to value them as human beings. They want you to like who they are and who they are becoming. They want you to really respect them.

"You have a front row seat when you are in business to helping people become the best version of themselves. When you help people see that they are likable, you really begin to show people their value. People are tired of being used and abused by selfish sales tactics and empty promises.

"Make it your goal to under promise and over deliver. Invite your clients out for coffee. Swing by their places of work and drop by a kind gift like a box of donuts (or for the more health conscious, a veggie or fruit tray). If you are going to spend money on your business, spend it on showing people that you genuinely like who they are and what they do.

"People not only want to be seen; they want to be known. They want to know there is something to like about them, and I'm going to challenge you to actually like them. You cannot fake authenticity. Look for the best qualities in your clients. You will undoubtedly have no problem seeing their faults. It takes a special kind of person to actually enjoy human beings.

"I hear it said all the time, 'My business would be so much easier if it weren't for people acting the way they do.'

The Sphere of Liking: The Attitude of Respect

Believe the best in people. Look for the silver lining. Reach for that intangible aspect of seeing not what people are, but what they can become. Respect what you have listened to and learned about them up to this point enough to enjoy them as human beings. Understand why they are the way they are and choose to like what you see!

"I remember as a child I was often told that I don't have to like people, I just had to love them. That sounds great. It even sounds admirable. But as I said before, people don't want to simply be tolerated, they want to be liked.

"There are enough messages that are communicated to people in their lifetimes that tell them they are not worthy, they are not valuable, and they are not liked just the way they are. Learn how to see beyond what you see when you encounter people.

"That high-maintenance client that is impossible to deal with? Yes, I want you to like them. That difficult client that doesn't listen to your advice? Yes, I want you to like them. That grumpy, negative client that always sees the glass half empty? Yes, I want you to like them, too.

"'Why?' you may ask.

"And here is my answer: because when you like people, you show them you respect them, even if they don't respect themselves enough to let you enter their process with them.

"This is the Sphere of Liking. It may be one of the most difficult spheres for you to learn how to dwell in. That's ok. I'm going to teach you how to enter the Sphere of Liking."

The 7 Spheres of a FriendMaker

LIKING

WORKSHOP NOTES

THE SPHERE OF LIKING

The goal of a FriendMaker in the Sphere of Liking is creating an enjoyable experience for your clients that ends with everyone having an attitude of *respect*. This requires detaching and adjusting. As Dave Sawyer says, "Reach for that intangible aspect of seeing not what people are, but what they can become." In this sphere, the goal is not simply tolerating people that annoy you, but actually respecting them enough to help them regardless of the payout for you.

Seeing people as human beings requires a level of detachment from your experience of them so that you can objectively help them with the process they are trying to mentally grasp for themselves. People are people. We must adjust ourselves and our expectations of people so that we can actually help them see a path forward when they see no path at all. I often tell my clients that I want to bring clarity for them of how to get where they want to be. I cannot bring clarity for them if I am emotionally wrapped up and affected by everything they are doing that grates against my own comfort level with certain personality types.

The Sphere of Liking: The Attitude of Respect

Stepping into this sphere is truly stepping out of our own comfort zone and engaging people where they are, not where we'd like them to be. We sometimes wish for different clients. We sometimes desire to work only with easy people. It's not difficult to like someone who is just like you. It takes a certain level of being uncomfortable to engage people in the Sphere of Liking.

Showing respect in the Sphere of Liking for a Friend-Maker shows up in three intentional practices:

1. Look for the good in people.
2. Take yourself less seriously.
3. Make them laugh through the process.

PRACTICE #1: LOOK FOR THE GOOD

Harsh Goenka, Indian billionaire and hotel magnate, was quoted as saying, "People are like books, some deceive you by their cover and others surprise you with their content."[20] This is an accurate description and a perfect metaphor for what you deal with when you encounter other human beings. There is so much to discover about people lurking beneath the surface of their sometimes hard or even unlikable exterior.

Entering into the Sphere of Liking requires that you look for the good in people. As Dave mentioned earlier, some people are more difficult to deal with than others. That doesn't mean that you should be intimidated or repelled by them. It just means that there may be more of a challenge dealing with some folks.

No matter what you see on the outside, there is always something to like about people. As you listen to people and learn what makes them who they are, you also must look for the best characteristics they present to you.

It takes a certain level of patience and vision to be able to serve people who are not like you and who you do not naturally take a liking to. People don't need you to see the negative front they sometimes put out there. They need you to look past that and see what could be. Your clients are secretly hoping that you will not be like everyone else they have encountered with regard to salespeople. They want to see that you are better than what they expect of someone in sales.

It doesn't make this an easy thing to do. In fact, as we have already noted, it may be the most difficult sphere to learn to dwell in because it really does require objectivity. We must recognize where we are already biased towards certain types of people. We have to overcome our own internal objections to how people are or how they choose to live, especially if they are different from us. The best salespeople know how to remain objective and not let their personal feelings get in the way of seeing the best in people.

PRACTICE # 2: TAKE YOURSELF LESS SERIOUSLY

There are endless quotes about learning how to take yourself less seriously. Brenden Burchard, author of *High-Performance Habits*, said, "Don't take yourself too seriously. Be the person who brings joy, humility and fun, even as you strive to reach difficult goals and make your difference."[21]

As a person who tends to spend too much time being serious in my own life, I have to take this practice more seriously! Life is too short to always be dealing with the heaviness of circumstances. There is plenty to be anxious about, stressed out about, and depressed about in this world we live in. And when people we are dealing with need a rest from all the seriousness of the ins and outs of this current transaction, we have to grow out of our need to always have the right answers for them in every situation. We have to take ourselves much less seriously than we do.

The Sphere of Liking: The Attitude of Respect

You are not the know-all, end-all of everything for your clients. Sometimes you have to take a step back from everything and breathe yourself.

Take a moment, even now, as you are reading this to stop and think on this one thought: When all is said and done, after this season of working with this one client, what will be the ultimate outcome of all the work you are doing? In the grand scheme of things, what you think is so serious right now will likely be a topic of conversation you and your colleagues or friends will laugh about later. You will more than likely be just fine when it's all said and done. And so will your client. Think about what life will be like on the other side of this difficult person and this difficult circumstance you are dealing with.

PRACTICE #3: MAKE YOUR CLIENT LAUGH

A few years ago, my family and I were in a tough situation. Financially we were in ruins, life was extremely difficult, and we didn't know day-to-day how life was going to turn out for us. Every day, it seemed, there was a new problem and a new obstacle for us to overcome. We were struggling in our circumstances, and we didn't see a way out.

Then, a dear friend, Steve, came over to drop off some food and offer us encouragement in the midst of our struggle. As we were chatting, Steve asked me if I had ever heard of a YouTuber named Ed Bassmaster. My wife and kids all gathered around the kitchen table as Steve pulled up video after video of this guy doing stupid things. I'll never forget how we laughed that night. Steve probably had places to go, but he hung out with us, and we just really enjoyed the time we had together. Laughter truly is the best medicine!

Sometimes, as I'm dealing with my clients over the long and sometimes arduous process of waiting for a real estate transaction to come to completion, I'll pop by their places of work or send them some off-the-wall text or meme that will get a laugh.

Learning to laugh with your client will endear you to them and will break the tension that sometimes exists with clients who are difficult to deal with. Make your client laugh. Do it often. Do it at the right time. Do it intentionally.

Dwelling in the Sphere of Liking doesn't have to be a chore. Make it fun.

Increase Your Respect

As you work through the Sphere of Liking, you will increase the respect level that people have for you as well as you have for them. Many times, liking people doesn't come naturally to us. We have our ways of dealing with life and sometimes it seems like others get in the way of us being able to cope with life the way we want to. When you see people as obstacles, you will only want to endure them, get around them, or rush through them.

Hurry is the enemy of respect. Hurry commoditizes people and doesn't not seek community. If we are not careful, getting things done will become our highest value and we will miss the opportunities along the way to enjoy the journey.

Business is a personal endeavor. We don't live so that we can work. We work so that we can live. That is our client's goal as well. I haven't met anyone who simply wants to work all the time and never have any time to enjoy the life they've been given.

If we can give ourselves fully to dwelling in the Sphere of Like, then we can find redemptive elements in the relationships with have with people we would normally consider too difficult to deal with. Once we spend time really getting to know the people we serve, we will find

The Sphere of Liking: The Attitude of Respect

ourselves growing to like them more. And when we like people, we show them we respect them.

Increase your respect for people by liking them. Look for the good in them. Take yourself less seriously. Make them laugh. Maybe, in time, you will find that what you didn't like about them originally was simply a mask that they wore until they felt comfortable enough with you to take it off. Once we listen, learn, and like people, we will grow in our ability to dwell in the next sphere of FriendMaking, the Sphere of Loyalty.

WORKSHOP SESSION #4
Be Loyal To Your Client

Chapter 10
The Sphere of Loyalty:
The Attitude of Advocacy

The seminar was buzzing after Dave introduced the first three spheres of a FriendMaker. Everyone was furiously taking notes and asking him lots of questions. Nolan pulled out his personal business journal and wrote down each attitude.

Attentiveness
Understanding
Respect

As he reviewed these attitudes, a pattern took shape. All the spheres pointed to an attitude that sought the benefit of the client over the benefit of the businessperson. Dave was teaching a selfless way of doing business. This was foreign to Nolan's experiences with most business trainings, which were about how to achieve success, gain notoriety, self-promote, and beat out the other guys.

In and of themselves, these things are not wrong or bad

to pursue. As a real estate agent, Nolan wanted to be successful. As a visible brand in his market, he wanted to be seen by the community as a "go-to" guy. As a businessman, it is very important to be able to promote yourself in your area of influence. And who doesn't want healthy competition?

Dave was quieting the room when he saw Nolan's hand go up. "Yes, Nolan? What is it, my friend?"

Nolan nervously replied, "Dave, I'm tracking with everything you are saying. I think it's all great stuff, and I want to be the kind of person who others see as attentive, understanding, and respectful. But what about personal success? What about increased visibility in the marketplace? What about self-promotion and healthy competition? Aren't these all valuable to businesspeople as well? How do we integrate all of this with the very real need to be profitable in business and to be able to make a good living doing our work? Is there room in the spheres for self-advancement? I mean, I don't want to be the selfish guy in the room, but I don't think anyone in this room is going to disagree with what I'm suggesting here. How does all of this help us make money?"

You could hear a pin drop as Nolan asked that last question. The other attendees at the workshop were nodding in agreement. Nolan continued, "Isn't the goal of business making money? I mean, how are we supposed to take care of our families while we are out here making friends?"

Dave grabbed a pen and wrote something down in his notebook. He paused for what felt like an entire minute, collecting his thoughts. "I'm glad you brought this up, Nolan. Usually, at some point in the conversation about friendmaking, the nuts and bolts of business building comes up. And you are right. You wouldn't be in business if you didn't have needs to be met. I don't know of a single businessperson who doesn't want to be successful, noticed

The Sphere of Loyalty: The Attitude of Advocacy

profitable, or competitive.

"Something I want you to take away from this workshop that is vital to your success in business is this one thought: *Profitability is a by-product of focusing on others first.* This workshop is about this very idea. Being a friend to your clients, your prospects, and your strategic business partners is how you help other people get what they want. By helping others, you will help yourself. I know it seems counterintuitive, but this is the truth. The more selfless you are, the more you are able to make progress for yourself and those you love. And that is what the Sphere of Loyalty is about, becoming an advocate for others. Let's dive in!"

LOYALTY

WORKSHOP NOTES

THE SPHERE OF LOYALTY

Dwelling in the Sphere of Loyalty is the next step in the progression of listening to, learning, and liking people. Being loyal is about developing an attitude of *advocacy* for people. Your client wants to know whether you are going to stick with them for the long haul. Too many businesspeople are 'fair-weather friends' with their clients. The minute the process becomes difficult, too often sales-

The 7 Spheres of a FriendMaker

people are ready to bail. This is the chief reason most small business don't last past the two-year mark. Problems mount up. Difficulties multiply. And the going gets tough.

Discomfort in a business deal is not a matter of if but when. You are going to face problems when dealing with your clients. Unpredictable forces are going to rear their ugly head at some point in your process with people. Anticipate problems. Expect difficulty. Understand that people don't enjoy conflict, confrontation, or complications. Everybody wants a smooth ride, but no journey is without its obstacles. Your job, as a FriendMaker in business, is to be ready for these pitfalls and to stand beside your clients as they navigate the difficulty of whatever is in front of them.

You have a choice when faced with complexity in your client relationship. You can either work *for* your client, or *against* them. What people need in times like this are advocates, not antagonists. That is where you enter the Sphere of Loyalty.

Becoming an advocate in the Sphere of Loyalty for a FriendMaker shows up in three intentional practices:

1. Show up.
2. Negotiate skillfully.
3. Fight for your clients.

PRACTICE #1: SHOW UP

Dave Sawyer, in his experience as a businessman, knows the importance of showing up for the people he works with. There are two ways to show up: showing up for the *short term* and showing up for the *long haul*. You need to develop this practice as well. Let me illustrate.

The Sphere of Loyalty: The Attitude of Advocacy

THE SHORT TERM

In a recent transaction I had with a seller, we were faced with a difficult decision in the short term. My seller had entered into a contract with a buyer who told us that they were going to purchase the home in "as-is" condition. The buyer asked for a home inspection so they could know more about the house.

In the course of the home inspection, the inspector flagged a plumbing problem as "severe" and "active." The buyer was very concerned. In reality, the problem was not as severe or as active as the home inspector's report had indicated. However, because it was a problem for the buyer, we had to address the issue swiftly and professionally. My seller wasn't happy because the buyer had offered to purchase the home in as-is condition, warts and all. We had a choice to make in that moment. We could insist the buyer keep his word and sign the contract on the house as it was, or we could try to alleviate the buyer's fears by calling a plumber out to look at the problem.

My seller chose to call the plumber, who found two minor leaks near the hot water heater in the home. He fixed one of the issues but left the other unfixed. The seller had to have the plumber out again to fix the other leak and then we submitted all the documentation to the buyer. After a series of conversations, documentation, and pictures, we found that the buyer was still unsatisfied with the fix. The home inspector's report had also questioned whether there was damage to the subfloor where the second repair had been done. While the issue in the home was minor, in the buyer's mind the issue was a major one.

My seller, in good faith, offered to not only have the repairs done, but also gave the buyer a credit of $1500 towards their closing costs in lieu of possible mitigation issues from the moisture the leaks had caused. Even after

The 7 Spheres of a FriendMaker

the repairs had been done and the money had been offered, the buyer was still worried about the issue. My seller was getting impatient with the buyer, for good reason. We had done above and beyond what was necessary to fix and address the issue, but the buyer wanted more documentation and peace of mind that they were not going to have a subfloor problem when they took possession of the home.

The plumber and the contractor we used to address the issues told us there was no subfloor damage. We had every right to say to the buyer, "We've done it all, there's nothing left to provide." In that moment, I had to show up for my client.

I told my seller that the missing piece for this buyer was a picture of the undamaged subfloor. In the end, my seller called the plumber out one more time to take down the insulation in the area of concern and take snapshots of the healthy subfloor for the buyer's sake.

"Showing up" took the form of having an honest conversation with my seller about the reality of this buyer's concerns. I had to advocate for my seller by asking them if they really wanted to sell their home or if this was a hill they wanted to die on. Speaking truth that was difficult for my seller to hear was the best way for me to advocate for them.

Because I told my seller the truth, the seller was able to create peace of mind for the buyer, and we ended up closing the deal at the end of that week.

THE LONG HAUL

Another example of showing up is being in your client's life long after the sale. In an Inman news article a few years back, Seth Godin was quoted as saying that, "91% of all realtors never contact the buyer or seller of a home after closing."[22] 91%! How loyal do you think your client will be to

The Sphere of Loyalty: The Attitude of Advocacy

you if you never talk to them, communicate with them, or reach out to them after you make your commission and walk away from their sale? We will discuss this more in the final sphere, but for now know that if you plan to build a business that lasts a lifetime, loyalty must first be shown to be earned. Showing up for people is the first step in dwelling in the Sphere of Loyalty. This will lead you to the second practice of advocacy: skillful negotiation.

PRACTICE #2: NEGOTIATE SKILLFULLY

Negotiation is an art. It requires understanding of the perspective of both sides of the argument. I often tell my sellers that they have to think like a buyer. Likewise, I tell my buyers that they have to put themselves in the shoes of the seller. Being able to remain objective is a major part of skillful negotiation. Sometimes it's like a poker game. You must hold your cards close so no one can see your hand. Other times, the best way forward is to lay your cards out on the table and let the other side know just where your client is.

This takes patience. It also requires emotional distance from the issue. People need to know that you are advocating for them, not getting emotionally involved. A skillful negotiator knows how to talk about the facts and not the intangibles. There is always uncertainty when people are purchasing a home or some other product or service but a skilled negotiator can always bring clarity by sticking to the facts.

Advocating for your clients in the Sphere of Loyalty is about showing up and skillfully negotiating. But the final step is the most important.

PRACTICE #3: FIGHT FOR YOUR CLIENTS

The best way to fight for your clients is to define the ultimate outcome of the scenario you find yourself in. As a

The 7 Spheres of a FriendMaker

businessperson, you must always keep the end result in mind. What is your client's ultimate goal? How can you show up and skillfully negotiate for your clients while moving the process in a direction that helps your client achieve their desired outcome?

The answer is to help your client pick the right battles. You must lay out for them the consequences of choosing a particular direction in the negotiation. If you pick the wrong hill to die on, the negotiation falls apart. But if you skillfully guide your client toward a decision that works in their favor, you are teaching your client that some battles are worth fighting and some are worth giving concessions.

The most difficult battles to fight for your clients are the ones where you know the ultimate outcome may be losing the deal in favor of starting over and finding someone else who will be easier to work with. Some people want you to give them everything and don't offer any concessions at all. As a businessperson, sometimes you have to be willing to lose the smaller battles so your client can win the larger war. This requires discernment and no small amount of education of the larger process.

It's often like playing chess. The stronger player is able to think two or three steps ahead of the other player. You must learn how to anticipate the possible moves of the other player. This requires patience, vision, strategy, and execution. Sometimes your client will make the right decision. Other times they will make the wrong decision. You must help your clients see all the possible outcomes of their decisions and help them navigate through the uncertainty of the process. Andy Andrews says, "God did not put in me the ability to always make the right decision, but he did give me the ability to make a decision and then make it right."[23]

Fighting for your clients is about owning your good decisions and your bad ones. Advocacy is about choosing

The Sphere of Loyalty: The Attitude of Advocacy

to remain loyal to your client and earning your client's loyalty as they trust you to help them navigate a complex process. Dwelling in the Sphere of Loyalty will help you earn that trust from your clients. This will inevitably lead you into a new sphere of friend making, the Sphere of Leaping.

WORKSHOP SESSION #5
Leap For Your Client

Chapter 11
The Sphere of Leaping:
The Attitude of Risk

After the first four sessions, everyone had a lot to discuss. Listening, learning, liking, and being loyal to their clients were not new ideas at all. As a matter of fact, the simplicity of Dave's seven spheres was not lost on anyone.

"We're past the halfway mark, folks!" Dave motioned for everyone to come close as he put the next slide on the screen. "Does anyone have any questions about what we've been talking about?"

Nolan raised his hand again. This time he wasn't afraid to ask the tough question. He knew this one was going to be good. "What do you do when you've been loyal to people, you've listened to them, learned them, liked them, and stayed completely loyal to them, and they don't end up being loyal to you? How do you handle it when you've spent time and money on people and then one day you find that they ended up using someone other than you for the service or product that you provide? How do you deal with this kind of a letdown? Is it ever ok for me to drop or

The 7 Spheres of a FriendMaker

sever the relationships I have pursued in my business if people don't reciprocate loyalty to me?"

Dave smiled again. "Well, Nolan, you've been bringing out the heavy guns today, haven't you? Those are all great questions! I want to address each of them, but first I want to ask if any of you here have experienced this. How did you handle it?"

A number of attendees told story after story of awkward customer experiences where they had invested in people and been disappointed by clients who they thought would be loyal to them, but who ended up going somewhere else. Nolan could tell that this question hit a nerve. Some people were emotional, even angry about the way they had been treated. As the difficulty of this subject became clear through people's stories, Dave interjected, "Quite honestly, folks, this is one of the most difficult aspects of client relationships. The truth is that people are fickle. They don't often know what they want. Many don't want advice or counsel. And way too many people are embarrassed to ask for help.

"You are going to face this reality throughout the life of your business, and it is going to be very important that you understand the proper way to handle this because there is a right way and a wrong way to handle clients who aren't loyal to you. Dealing with people as friends is risky business, isn't it? Let's take a quick rabbit trail and talk about three ways to handle disloyalty. This will be helpful before we move into our next sphere."

The Three Cs of Reconciliation

"When you find out, either directly or indirectly, about a past client who has decided to use a different vendor than you, take a moment and try the three Cs of client reconciliation: consider, collect, and confront."

The Sphere of Leaping: The Attitude of Risk

Dave wrote these words out on the board in front of everyone.

- Consider
- Collect
- Confront

"The first step in reconciling with a client is to *consider their situation*. You don't have all the facts. And often the first response we have is a selfish response. We feel slighted. We feel betrayed. We have to take a step back and consider what we know of our client. We also need to assess what kind of a relationship we have actually built with them. If the only communication they ever got from us was a random phone call every once in a blue moon, how can we expect them to be loyal to us? Were we consistent in our communication? Were we present when they needed us? How loyal were we to them? We must consider our part in the relationship and whether we gave as much as we thought we did.

"The second step is *collecting information*. We must do our homework about their situation. This will involve looking back at our interactions with them over time. It will also require communication from us to them. We can email them or text them to let them know we know they have moved on, but let's be honest, the best way to collect information at this point is going to be through a simple phone call or a personal visit. Maybe they were embarrassed to talk to us. Perhaps there was a family relationship they felt obliged to work with over you. Sometimes people just don't know how to communicate with you that they wanted to use you but just weren't able to. All of this leads us to our final step of reconciliation.

"*Confront your client.* Now, when I say *confront*, what I don't mean is a negative interaction. I mean that you need to graciously give them an out and the benefit of the doubt. Ask them how they are doing. Ask them whether there is anything you can help them with. And ultimately wish them well as they move on from you. You can find out indirectly what their motive was, and oftentimes you can salvage the relationship by letting them know that your friendship with them is not dependent on them always using you as their preferred vendor. That being said, you can also ask them how you can better serve them if given the opportunity in the future. It's important to be sensitive to the individual circumstance and not push too quickly or prod too personally if you meet resistance. Confronting someone doesn't have to be an awkward, shaming experience. In fact, clearly communicating with people will lead to a deeper trust and may offer you hope for a future business relationship with them.

"It is very important for each of us to understand that some people don't have the capacity to give or receive the kind of friendship I am describing in my FriendMaker workshop. Relationships are messy and unpredictable, but I believe that the risk involved in doing business this way is worth it. But there is another aspect to all of this that I want to address.

"You can give people the benefit of the doubt, and sometimes it will work out positively. But sometimes you find that your loyalty to others doesn't always end up with them reciprocating that same kind of loyalty. Especially in business interactions. Sometimes your competitor is cheaper, easier, or more attractive than you. And there is nothing you can do to compete with that if your client chooses to go in that direction.

"Steve Harvey once said, 'Loyalty has an expiration date. The problem is when you're the nice person your loyalty lasts far longer to certain people than it should. Because their loyalty to you has been expired. But you, being a good person, you hang on to friendships and become forgiving far longer than you really should be. Loyalty has an expiration date.'"[24]

The Sphere of Leaping: The Attitude of Risk

The room stood quiet for a moment as Dave shared. "As you do your business, and as you make friends with your clients, you must rate the quality of the relationships you have with your clientele. Some people will remain loyal to you no matter what you do. These are your top tier clients. Some people will remain loyal to you as long as you consistently show up in their lives, offer them valuable information, or stay present in their mind. These are your secondary tier clients. Some people will only remain loyal if you give them something in return; if you stop giving, they will stop being your client. And finally, some people will not be loyal to you no matter what you do.

"You will have to rate where you think the people in your life stand with regard to their loyalty to you. This is not to say that you can't still be loyal to people, reach out to people, stay in contact with them, or even keep them on your mailing list. It just means that you must recognize the ones who see the value in your relationship with them. Some people don't see the value and never will. Focus on those who do."

Dave continued, "It's so interesting that your question came up at this time, Nolan. The next sphere we are talking about is my favorite one because this is where you really step into the fight and take big risks for the sake of the people who are loyal to and value you.

"I want to talk about vulnerability and taking risks. Vulnerability is often seen as a weakness in business, but I want to challenge that notion. I submit to you that it is one of your biggest strengths in the client relationship. Here's why.

"As business owners, we oftentimes want to put up a front with our clients that we know it all and can handle all their questions. We think people want us to always know the answers, but the reality is that we don't always know the answers to our clients' questions, and we often aren't

The 7 Spheres of a FriendMaker

prepared for the uncertainty that arises in the middle of clients' transactions.

"How are we supposed to handle this?" Dave asked.

"Fake it till you make it!" quipped someone.

Dave furrowed his brow. Everyone held their breath. "That is not a good position to take, and I'll tell you why." Dave got really quiet. "We are going for integrity here. People want to know that the business owner they are working with isn't just winging it. While there may be times that we take risks in our communication with our clients, the last thing you want is to take a risk that costs you a relationship because you were dishonest. If you don't know something, here's my best advice: *own it*.

"There is an age-old adage that goes, 'People don't care how much you know until they know how much you care.' Have you ever heard this? Folks, it is true!

"Now let me clarify something about the difference between vulnerability and lack of confidence. You can be both confident with your clients and vulnerable with them at the same time. And the way you do that is through honesty and education.

"There may not be anything more important in relationships than honesty. Without honesty you can't have trust. And without trust, your relationship doesn't stand to last.

"I want you to have lasting relationships with your clients in your business. If friendship is the foundation of all good business, then trust is the foundation of all good friendships. And you cannot have trust without honesty. Becoming a FriendMaker is about proving to people that you are trustworthy and that there is value in linking themselves to you."

The Sphere of Leaping: The Attitude of Risk

LEAPING

WORKSHOP NOTES

THE SPHERE OF LEAPING

Educating your clients about the process, the inevitable pitfalls, and all the possible outcomes is important. Setting proper expectations and clearly communicating that your clients should expect obstacles is one great way of educating them and thereby creating confidence in your skills as their trusted advisor. You don't need to know everything. You just need to know how to keep calm and press on when the going gets tough. You need the ability to solve problems. Real estate sales trainer & business coach Sean Carpenter has built his business on three indispensable ideas: "Building Relationships, Solving Problems, and Having Fun."[25] If you can do these three things in business, you will succeed because people want to be known, they want skilled professionals helping them, and they want to enjoy the process and the results! Entering the Sphere of Leaping allows you to do these things with your clients.

Becoming a risk-taking FriendMaker in the Sphere of Leaping shows up in three intentional practices:

The 7 Spheres of a FriendMaker

1. Always tell the truth.
2. Go deep with people.
3. Give 110%.

PRACTICE #1 – ALWAYS TELL THE TRUTH

The controversial English author George Orwell has been credited by some sources as saying, "In a time of universal deceit, telling the truth is a revolutionary act."[26] Whoever said it, I believe this to be true. At a time where trust in some of our society's authority structures can be perceived as eroding, it is interesting to note that trust in business itself has actually begun to increase worldwide over the past few years. People want to trust in your business.

Public relations firm Daniel J. Edelman Holdings, Inc evaluates the trends in business, government, media, and non-government organizations (NGOs). On their website, Edelman has written an outstanding piece titled "20 Years of Trust" which follows the rise and fall of trust in all four of these public sectors over the last twenty years. On one section of the site, Edelman hones in on this truth:

> "We cannot live only for ourselves," wrote Herman Melville, the author of Moby Dick. "A thousand fibers connect us with our fellow men; and among those fibers, as sympathetic threads, our actions run as causes, and they come back to us as effects." Trust is the tie that binds us in our shared quest for a better future.[27]

It is interesting to note that above news media and government, business is esteemed as more competent and trustworthy, while non-government agencies are considered to be the most ethical, but not as competent as businesses. What this tells me is that people want to trust in your business if you'll just answer the integrity question for them.

The Sphere of Leaping: The Attitude of Risk

Not only do they want to trust in your business, they also want to know that if they put their trust in your business, you will go to bat for them. Honesty is the starting point. Dave Sawyer alludes to this in his workshop when he says, "Without honesty you can't have trust. And without trust, your relationship doesn't stand to last."

The Sphere of Leaping is a space in your relationship with your client where you have developed such a trust with them that they believe you will go above and beyond the call of duty to fight for them. The foundation for this kind of relationship is telling the truth. Truth-telling between you and your clients joins you together in such a way that trust and confidence in your loyalty to them is established.

The Spheres of Loyalty and Leaping are closely intertwined because they both require a consistent level of advocacy and risk. You need to fight for your clients and make yourself vulnerable with them by being honest. This will open you up to going deep—not just wide—with your clients.

PRACTICE # 2 - GO DEEP WITH PEOPLE, NOT JUST WIDE

My referral sources have shown me that the same people tend to refer business to me over and over. Instead of trying to scale my business by quickly adding more clientele, I have chosen to go deep with the few clients I already have so that I can mine the business that is in their referrals. What most of us don't like about this is that it is a slower pace than what many of us would prefer.

But what I have also found as I have chosen to go deeper with people is that they know I am willing to be vulnerable with them about the things that I am most concerned about in my business. I am able to tell them when I'm worried about future business or something that

The 7 Spheres of a FriendMaker

is going on in my personal life. I give them insight into what makes me tick and how I can better serve them. It seems counterintuitive, but by going deep with a few, you take on greater risk, but you also reap a greater reward of relationship.

Many people in business choose to scale wide and go an inch deep, and their businesses suffer when the going gets tough because they didn't do the hard work of building a solid base of relationships with their clientele. When the next recession hits or the next economic downturn happens, they will struggle to keep themselves afloat because their business was built on the superficial transactional relationships of the many rather than the deep relational connections with the few.

I'm not suggesting that you can't scale your business, but I do suggest that as you go wide with clients, you maintain a level of depth. Don't sacrifice quality of relationships for more profits. Wait. Be patient. Slow down. Let the connections you have go deeper and slowly go wider as time and relationship permits. You will get there eventually.

PRACTICE #3 - GIVE 110%, LEAVE NOTHING FOR THE TRIP BACK

When I worked for my friend Chris Garrett at Weichert Realtors in Murfreesboro a few years ago, I was just learning how to build a pipeline of business. It was important to me to be able to assess how much risk I was taking on with each client. I knew that not every client would make it to close. Worried about this reality, I once asked him how many of his contracts he expected to make it across the finish line. He told me, "All of them. Every time I get a buyer or a seller into a contract, I expect it to close."

That is the mindset of someone who plans to succeed. As Earl Nightingale once said, "Success is the progressive

The Sphere of Leaping: The Attitude of Risk

realization of a worthy goal or ideal."[28] When you leap for your client, you must operate under the assumption that you are progressively moving your client all the way to victory. Curveballs inevitably are thrown and you just have to keep swinging. Your clients will know if you have the confidence of a winner or if your insecurities are guiding their process. Expect the best. Prepare for the worst. And give 110%.

In his book The Last Arrow, Erwin McManus retells the story of one of his favorite movies, Gattaca, with Ethan Hawke, Jude Law, and Uma Thurman. In the story, set in the future, Ethan Hawke's character, Vincent, is a natural born human in a world of elite, genetically predisposed superhumans. Throughout the movie, the contrast is made between him and his superhuman brother and their efforts to swim across a channel at night. His brother, the superior swimmer, wins time and time again. Until the end of the movie. Then we see Vincent beat his brother in an impossible feat of strength. His reason when asked by his brother how he did it is something for us to ponder: "You want to know how I did it, Anton? I never saved anything for the swim back!"

McManus then tells us,

> If failure is our inevitable future, then let's fail boldly and fail forward. But whatever happens, let's not hide behind the excuse that we didn't give it everything we had. Perhaps the life we long for is beyond the point of no return. That thought has never left me: that he never saved anything for the way back. This mind-set, I am convinced, is the fundamental difference between those who strike the arrow three times and those who strike until they've used the last arrow. They leave nothing for the way back. They save nothing for the next life.[29]

The 7 Spheres of a FriendMaker

For us as FriendMakers, this mindset must be in the way we leap for our clients. We must save nothing for the swim back. We must jump in with both feet and head for the other shore with the attitude that in risking everything in relationship we will get our clients to the other side.

If you don't think you can make it, don't jump in the water. But if you believe in yourself and are confident that you can move your client into the next sphere, the Sphere of Leadership, then jump right in and swim like you've got nothing left to lose!

WORKSHOP SESSION #6
Lead Your Client

Chapter 12
The Sphere of Leading:
The Attitude of Service

Everyone came back from the break after Dave was through with the Sphere of Leaping and found this Lao Tzu quote written on Dave's whiteboard:

> "A leader is best when
> people barely know he exists,
> when his work is done, his aim fulfilled,
> they will say: we did it ourselves." [30]

Dave stood up and began. "John Maxwell once said years ago, 'Everything rises and falls on leadership.' The way you have served your client up until this point in your relationship will either give you the right to lead them or it will have convinced your client that you are not worth following in this process. Much of what we have been talking about in this seminar has been focused on *care*. Something I haven't spoken much about is something that is of equal importance: *competence*.

"It has been said by many coaches, business gurus, and

The 7 Spheres of a FriendMaker

trainers the world over that 'it's the skills that pay the bills.' I want to take a moment and talk to you about your competence as a salesperson. You can listen to your clients, learn them, like them, be loyal to them, and leap for them, but if you cannot lead them well, then all of your effort will be for nothing.

"Leadership is influence through service and skills. In effect, it is care *and* competence. You must care for your clients, but you must also be able to get them from point A to point B.

"I chose this sphere to be near the end because it is true that people don't care how much you know until they know how much you care… but in the end, they still care about your knowledge, your skills, and your competency level. You can make friends all you want, but if you can't deliver when it's game time, you won't be able to keep clients coming through your doors. Be good at what you do."

Everyone was nodding at this point. So many of them knew all of this friend-making stuff was good in theory. Dave continued, "The key is to lead people in such a way that they feel confident in the strides they are taking to walk through the process you've laid out for them. You need to get some experience in your craft before you can lead people through the process of buying or selling whatever your specialty is.

"Finally, you have to be able to teach people how to think like the person on the other side of the product or service you are selling. For example, when I sit down with a client for the first time, one of the first things I tell them is, 'As a buyer, I want you to put yourself in the shoes of the person you are trying to purchase a home from.' Likewise, if a person is selling a home, I tell them to think like a buyer. Help your clients ask questions of the other side to find out the best way to serve them.

The Sphere of Leading: The Attitude of Service

WORKSHOP NOTES

THE SPHERE OF LEADING

Dwelling in the Sphere of Leading is all about serving other people. If you have the notion that you are trying to convince them of something that they don't want to be convinced of, you'll lose them every time. But if you can create in their mind the belief that you are there to serve them powerfully, then you will be able to lead them into a journey of self-discovery and also how to win if faced with multiple offers or just a difficult party on the other side. Money talks, but sometimes there are other factors besides money that motivate people to work with you.

Becoming a servant in the Sphere of Leading for a FriendMaker shows up in three intentional practices:

1. Know your craft inside and out.
2. Provide wise counsel based on your experiences.
3. Model an attitude of servanthood.

PRACTICE #1 - KNOW YOUR CRAFT INSIDE AND OUT

There's no substitute for being good at your job. When

The 7 Spheres of a FriendMaker

you are providing services or products for the general public, you must be able to present those services and products with excellence. Winning basketball coach Pat Riley once said, "Excellence is the gradual result of always striving to do better."[31] Gain knowledge of your craft. Become the best in your field at what you do. Attend the trainings, get the skills, and practice, practice, practice. Practice doesn't make perfect, but it sure does help.

Back in the 1970s there was a trainer named Noel Burch with a company called Gordon Training International who developed the Conscious Competence Ladder/Matrix (see Fig. 9).[32] In this matrix we can see a visual representation of the process we all go through when we are new at something. We move from a place where we don't know what we don't know all the way around the matrix to the place where we unconsciously act with skill and competence in our chosen area of expertise.

Let's take a moment and go through this matrix together. I think it will help you better understand where you are in your ability to do your job and maybe help you craft a plan to get to a place where you can do it, with excellence, without having to think about it.

<u>Level One - Unconscious & Unskilled</u> - "I don't know WHAT I don't know."

When we are in this stage of learning, we are both ignorant and incompetent. In order to gain knowledge, we have to run through the process a few times and begin to gain *experience*. Experience is the key to developing skills. Eventually our experience turns into a habit that becomes second nature to us.

<u>Level Two - Conscious & Unskilled</u> - "I know THAT I don't know."

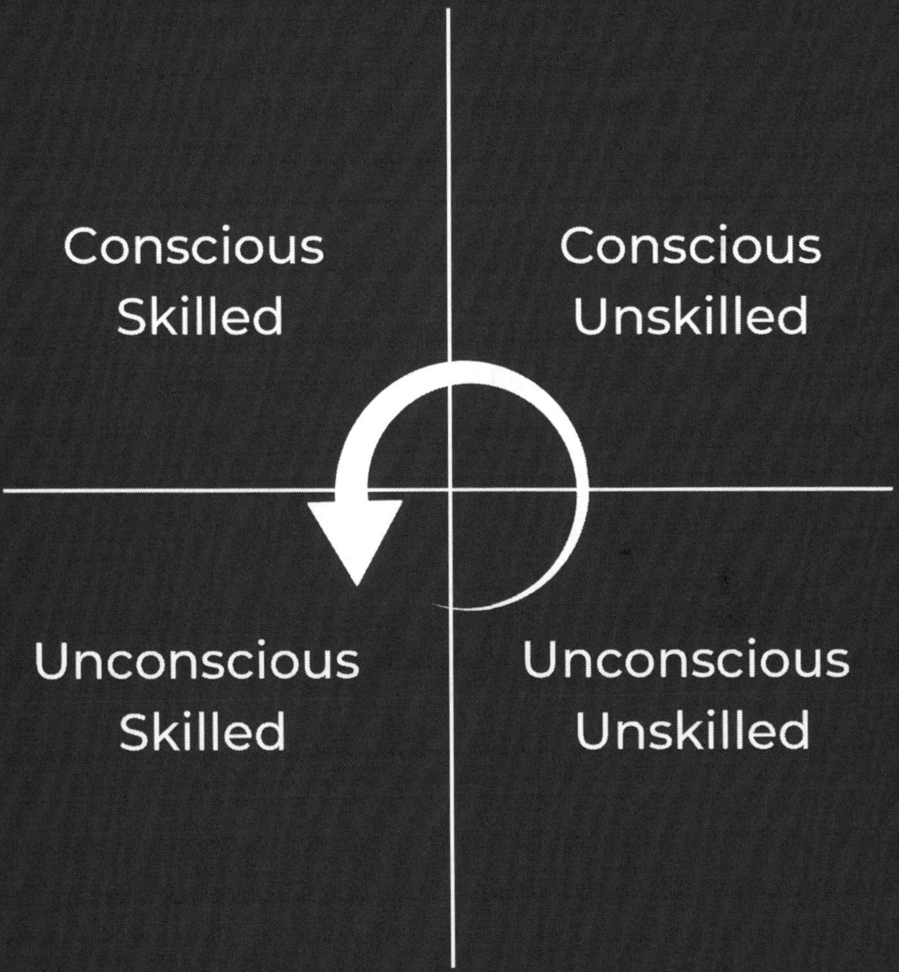

Conscious Skilled	Conscious Unskilled
Unconscious Skilled	Unconscious Unskilled

Fig. 9 [33]

The 7 Spheres of a FriendMaker

At this stage in our training, we are at least aware of our inability to do something. We know that we don't have the skills necessary to complete the task at hand, but with this self-awareness we have the humility to say, "I know what I don't know." With the help of a mentor, we can gain the experience needed to move into the next level.

<u>Level Three - Conscious & Skilled</u> - "I know AND I know."

Once we reach this level, our confidence level is up and the temptation to become arrogant is very real. But if we hold onto some humility and continue to practice our craft with excellence, we will be able to eventually do things without thinking about them. Again, this all takes time, mentoring, experience, and practice, practice, practice. With this knowledge and experience, we eventually move into the final level of conscious competence.

<u>Level Four - Unconscious & Skilled</u> - "I don't know THAT I know."

This final stage is about being so experienced and skilled that we have muscle memory and are able to just do what we do without thinking about it that much. The temptation here is to just coast and not communicate well with our clients or those we are training. We know our job so well that it is second nature to us.

Ultimately, knowing these different stages of learning will help us to recognize that learning our craft and doing what we do with excellence is a process that takes time. But once we have achieved a level of unconscious competence, we can confidently lead people through the sales process and offer our insights, wisdom, and experiences to help them navigate through.

PRACTICE # 2 - PROVIDE WISDOM BASED ON EXPERIENCE

The Sphere of Leading: The Attitude of Service

As we master our craft, we can become an excellent source of wisdom and counsel for our clients. Dwelling in the Sphere of Leading as a FriendMaker is so important because we can lead our clients into and through the process of purchasing our product or hiring us for our service. We have earned the right to be followed by them because we showed them that we care about them and have the skills and competence to lead them into the future.

When I first became a realtor, I didn't know what I didn't know. It wasn't until I had led a few clients through the sales process that I had the experience necessary to help my next clients navigate through the same process with clarity and confidence. It also became possible to set proper expectations with my clients. Being able to foresee obstacles and lay out for them their options was very valuable. When you are confident in your ability to help them navigate through the uncertainty of the sales process, it leaves more room for you to handle the unknowns and the intangibles that come with being in an ever-changing market. Problems always arise, but the wise and experienced salesperson can draw upon the past to help their clients in the future. You just have to be willing to make mistakes and learn from them.

When you don't know something, learn how to lean on the expertise of more experienced and knowledgeable mentors. There are always plenty of others who have been right where you are. Learn from their mistakes and implement their strategies into your business model so that you don't have to make the same mistakes. If you don't have experience, the only way to solve that problem is to get more experience! So, make your mistakes, learn from them, and use that knowledge to help your clients keep from making mistakes of their own.

PRACTICE # 3 - MODEL A SERVANT'S HEART

Finally, and most importantly, model a servant's heart

The 7 Spheres of a FriendMaker

with your clients. A servant doesn't act like they know something they don't know. They just serve until they get it right.

Teach your clients how to think. I know this seems redundant, but it truly matters that your people can put themselves in the other party's position. There is a lot of wisdom in this strategy. There is also a humility that comes in helping people create a smooth path to close for their opposing side.

By teaching your clients how to think about the other party, you accomplish three important goals:

Goal #1 - Knowledge of the sales process
Goal #2 - Ability to navigate uncertainty with confidence
Goal #3 - Helping your client get what they want

All of this must be done with an attitude of humility. One of the marks of a true FriendMaker is selflessness. Just because you know more than your client doesn't mean you have to make them feel stupid in your presence. In fact, it should be just the opposite. Knowing more than your client about your craft should create in them a respect for your profession as well as a healthy respect for the relationship you seek to build with them.

When people are convinced that you are in their corner and they know you are a capable professional, they will allow you to lead them through the sales process. It also sets you up to dwell in the final sphere of FriendMaking which is the Sphere of Loving.

WORKSHOP SESSION #7
Love Your Client

Chapter 13
The Sphere of Loving:
The Attitude of Care

The final session was about to begin and Nolan knew that what Dave was sharing was going to change everything about the way he did business. He knew that he couldn't continue to see his work as just finding the next transactions, making the next sale, or trying to convince his next prospect to use him to provide his services. He also knew that what Dave was proposing was going to be hard work. Digging into relationship building is both mentally and emotionally difficult. What Dave had shared so far was eye-opening because it was so simple and still very true. Nolan now understood that authentic friendship truly is the foundation of every good business practice.

Dave walked to the front of the room and wrote one word on the white board.

LOVE

"I don't know of a more important word in the human

The 7 Spheres of a FriendMaker

language than the word love," Dave began. "It is the most talked about, sung about, and written about word in any language. Many people have tried to define it, but all the definitions seem to fall short. We all want love, but most of us don't know how to obtain it. We all feel it from time to time in our lives, but most of us wonder if what we felt was truly love or something else. It is elusive, intangible, and confusing to more and more people as we all try to discover and journey into its depths.

"I'm not going to attempt to define love or to explain how you can obtain it," Dave continued. "But what I would like to do is to introduce to you the Sphere of Loving as the final and most important sphere to learn to dwell in.

"The main attitude for you as you seek to dwell within this sphere is that of care. You cannot love folks well if you don't stay in touch with them after you sell them your product or service. People long for connection. Because of this, the one characteristic that you can implement in your business that will create connection with your clients is that of a consistent plan of after-the-sale client care. *Your business will either thrive or die depending on your system of outward communication with your past clients.* Taking people through the process of the first six spheres will show your client how great it is to work with you while they are in the process of purchasing your product or service. But entering the Sphere of Loving will take you and your client into a new level of relationship, one of referrals and repeat business.

"It is my hope that as you internalize each of the spheres, develop the attitudes that each sphere encourages, and put into your life the intentional practices that each sphere demands, you will find yourself becoming the kind of person that others will want to do business with. Not only that, but I also believe that when people want to do business with you, they will also share you with their friends, co-workers, family, neighbors, and others within their spheres of influence."

The Sphere of Loving: The Attitude of Care

LOVING

WORKSHOP NOTES

THE SPHERE OF LOVING

Dave's spheres of friend making have taken us full circle through the entire sales process. Now that you've been through the process with your client—you've listened to them, learned them, liked (or attempted to like) them, been loyal to them, leaped for them, and led them—you are going to want to show your clients that you love them. As Dave says, "I don't know of a more important word in the human language than the word *love*."

Becoming care-ful in the Sphere of Loving for a Friend-Maker shows up in three intentional practices:

1. Reward their trust.
2. Developing a system of after-the-sale client care.
3. Follow up consistently."

PRACTICE #1 - REWARD YOUR CLIENT'S TRUST

The first practice we must use to dwell in the Sphere of Love is to reward our client's trust in us. Something great

The 7 Spheres of a FriendMaker

happened when we sold our product or service to our client: we were able to help them get what they wanted! Because they trusted us in the sales process, we now have the opportunity to show our appreciation to them and communicate our intentions beyond the sale. This requires a basic understanding of how to show love to them.

American author, speaker, and radio show host Gary Chapman became famous in 1992 for writing a groundbreaking book entitled The Five Love Languages. In this book, Chapman identified five primary ways people give and receive love to one another.

The Five Love Languages are as follows:

- Acts of service
- Receiving gifts
- Quality time
- Words of affirmation
- Physical touch [34]

Rewarding people for their trust involves different methods for different kinds of clients. Hopefully, after spending time with your clients in the other spheres, you've gotten to know them pretty well. Your knowledge of your client is going to come in very handy here.

If you are a retail provider who sells products like baked goods or articles of clothing, you will likely have to deal with your clients differently than if you are a service provider who provides services like financial advice or mortgage lending. However you work for your clients, it will be important for you to remember *who they are, what you learned about them* when you worked with them, and how best to communicate your appreciation for their trust in you.

The Sphere of Loving: The Attitude of Care

Acts of Service

If you are a retail provider, rewarding the client whose primary love language is acts of service may look like doing something kind for them or for someone they value. You could create a reward that benefits the client or someone else in a charitable way that, when a client purchases your product, a portion of the proceeds of your sales could go to benefit those less fortunate. You would just need to be sure to communicate that to your clientele.

If you are a service provider, reward a client who speaks this love language by offering to help them move into their home or by adding one of your services for free that you normally charge for. Anything that communicates that you desire to serve your client is going to be the best way for you to show love to these folks.

Receiving Gifts

For retail providers and service providers, this could be as simple as giving your client a gift card or a coupon to use in the future. Depending on the size and nature of the sale, you may want to give in proportion to the amount of time, money, or relational connection you had with your client. Giving gifts doesn't have to be a one-size-fits-all approach. Just remember that certain industries do have limits on gifts, so be sure to know the laws associated with your particular industry and gift-giving. There is a difference between genuine appreciation of your clients and bribing people for personal gain. Obviously, I discourage the latter!

When all is said and done, giving your client a tangible gift is often the best way to communicate your love and appreciation to them no matter what love language they prefer. Just make sure the gift matches the personality of the client.

The 7 Spheres of a FriendMaker

Quality Time

Some people just enjoy the pleasure of your company. For retail providers, this may pose some difficulty because the nature of retail sales is often short and sweet while the nature of most service providers happens over the course of the sales process. Either way, you want to communicate that you appreciate people by creating environments where they can get to know you and some of your other clients better.

I have seen many businesspeople throw parties and events where their clients can come in, grab something to eat, dance, have conversation, and just enjoy themselves on a Friday night or during lunch on a Tuesday afternoon. The way we connect is face-to-face. With that in mind, quality time can be done one-on-one over coffee or in a medium or large event space with a group of people.

Words of Affirmation

People who communicate love this way really enjoy kind words spoken in appreciation. This can be done verbally or via text, email, or most especially through a personal handwritten note. Sometimes there is no substitute for simply speaking kind words to people as you go all the way through the process. You have been their coach, now it is time to be their friend.

Physical Touch

I don't have to warn you about the dangers of inappropriate contact with your clients throughout the sales process or afterward. It can be difficult to express love to your clients in this way, but that doesn't diminish the importance of using this love language to communicate to people. Offering a handshake, a hug, or a gentle pat on the back can go a long way to communicate to the person whose primary love language is physical touch.

The Sphere of Loving: The Attitude of Care

Look people directly in the eyes when you speak with them. Allow yourself to connect with them on a deeper level by showing them appreciation through appropriate forms of touch as you finish up your time with them. You show people you love them by appreciating the value they have placed on you by trusting you to help them get what they want.

PRACTICE #2 - DEVELOP A SYSTEM OF AFTER-THE-SALE CLIENT CARE

The next practice that FriendMakers need to develop in the Sphere of Loving is a system of client care that outlasts the process of the sale. If you want to be consistent in the care of your client long after you sell your product or provide your service, you need to have a system of care and appreciation in place.

The best systems include regular outward communication to your clients through phone calls, handwritten notes, and personal visits to your client's homes or workplaces with a small gift of appreciation. It is not my intent with this book to reinvent the wheel with these strategies, only to make you aware of them and the power that doing them consistently can generate in referral business for you as you continue to love your client's consistency long after the sale.

1. Phone Calls - The Goal: Genuine Connection.

Look at your phone contact list. More than likely, you put those names in your phone because at some point you thought those people were worthy of keeping their phone number. In sales, those names and numbers, emails and addresses are the beginnings of your personal database of referral sources for your business. Those people are your friends or at least your strategic business partners. You keep in touch with people by simply calling them to check in, see how they are doing, and let them know you care about them and their life. Developing a systematic way of staying in touch with your database through a monthly or quarterly phone call is the first step in showing your clients you care beyond the sale. Asking them how they are enjoying their product or service that you provided is a sure way to communicate care and concern to your people.

2. Handwritten Notes - The Goal: Genuine Gratitude

We live in a digital age, a fast-paced society, and an increasingly impersonal world. What better way to bridge the gap with people than writing them a personal greeting or thank-you note every once in a while? Most residential mail for people comes in the form of bills and advertisements. When people receive a handwritten note in the mail from you, it communicates something different. It reminds people that they are human and that you thought enough of them to take a minute of your time to write them a note. If you have a plan to write notes to people every time you see them or interact with them, you will develop relational equity which will go a long way in the sales process in the future or for future referrals your client may send you.

3. Personal Visits - The Goal: Genuine Relationship

The sky is the limit on the kind of personal visits you can do with your clients. Because each client is unique and has their own way of going about life, you have to tailor your personal visits to the kinds of clients you have. Some of your clients will be small business owners, and you might want to swing by their businesses with a box of donuts and a handful of your cards. Some of your clients work in an office, so you may want to create a number of small pop-by gifts to hand out in their workroom. Others may be retired and living at home. You may want to bring something small by their homes once a quarter to let them know you are still available to help with anything they may need at any time. Any way you look at it, you'll have plenty of oppo-

The Sphere of Loving: The Attitude of Care

rtunities to connect in face-to-face relationship with your clients, you just need to do the final practice: follow up.

PRACTICE #3 - FOLLOW UP CONSISTENTLY

The largest hurdle in dwelling in the Sphere of Loving with the attitude of care comes down to consistency. It is not in human nature to follow up. This is the reason people begin the new year with the intention to work out but quit four weeks in. This is the reason people who start a new diet can usually only make it a few days before falling away. This is the reason new converts to an idea or religion end up losing faith and walking out on their commitments.

Fortunately, follow up doesn't have to be difficult. Discipline doesn't have to be elusive. In my experience, follow up is about putting into practice two important ideas in your personal development: discipline and accountability. These two ideas are a necessary part of being the kind of person people want to do business with for the long haul. Let's explore them more closely.

Personal Discipline

In his book Atomic Habits, James Clear says, "Every goal is doomed to fail if it goes against the grain of human nature." Human nature is undisciplined, unmotivated, and largely unchanged, but Clear offers hope by outlining "a simple set of rules we can use to build better habits. They are (1) make it obvious, (2) make it attractive, (3) make it easy, and (4) make it satisfying."[35]

When we set goals and develop habits that help us follow up with our clients, we put into practice things that will help us become consistent in staying in touch with our clients. This means clarifying which forms of outward communication we intend to use and then coming up with a plan for how to implement them.

The 7 Spheres of a FriendMaker

- **Make it obvious:** We set obvious goals like "I am going to make 10 phone calls today. I'm going to write 5 handwritten notes today. I'm going to visit 5 past clients this week.
- **Make it attractive:** We give ourselves a reward for accomplishing the goal. For example, "When I finish making my 5 social media interactions today, today, I'll go get a cup of coffee at Starbucks." This makes doing our work more fun and gives us the gratification of reaching a small goal.
- **Make it easy:** Create a goal that is attainable in a short period of time. Don't tell yourself you have to call twenty people if you know that the average phone conversation lasts a half an hour and you only have eight hours a day to talk to people. Set goals you can actually reach.
- **Make it satisfying:** Nobody wants to accomplish goals that don't mean anything. Perhaps the most powerful idea in Clear's book is that developing habits is not about "*having* something... (but) about *becoming* someone."[36] This is the main idea of becoming a FriendMaker. The satisfying thing about achieving your goals is when you genuinely connect with another human being. Whatever you do, do it with purpose and passion. You can't put a price tag on authentic human connection. This is satisfying on several different levels.

Professional Accountability

In addition to personal discipline, we must have some form of accountability. In an office environment, that is often the boss or manager. But when you are trying to do more than just your job, hiring a professional business coach to help you determine what your goals are, give you accountability in developing your communication habits, and continually encourage you to reevaluate your progress is absolutely critical. If we want to develop consistency in following up with our clients over the long haul, we must remember that we cannot do this alone.

The Sphere of Loving: The Attitude of Care

There are several great business coaches in the different industries. I encourage you to find someone local who specializes in your particular industry. Interview a few before you commit to one, and try them out for at least three months to begin with. Commit to a coaching relationship long enough to see the benefits of it, and give yourself time to grow in your business.

Rome wasn't built in a day; neither are strong, relational businesses. It always takes time to earn people's trust and to grow into the person you want to become. Walt Disney once said, "Do what you do so well that they will see it and want to bring their friends."[37] FriendMakers know that working at their craft with excellence and following up with their clients by consistently loving, communicating, and staying in touch with their clients will result in successful businesses as well as friendships that will last a lifetime. Ultimately, this is what being a FriendMaker is all about.

Epilogue
Beyond Business

Six months had passed by since Nolan had attended Dave's FriendMaker workshop. In that time, Nolan had begun to approach his relationships with prospective clients, friends, and strategic business partners from a new perspective. He began leaning into the Seven Spheres of a FriendMaker in every relationship he had, and it was paying off.

He remembered that *friendship is the foundation of all good business practice*, so he began to look at people as potential friendships, not potential sales. He focused first on getting to know the people he already had listed in his contacts on his phone. He figured that this made the most sense because these people were already folks he felt important enough to put into his phone.

He also remembered that *success is more than just a quick rise to the top*. A lot of phone calls and notes were sent during this time, reconnecting with people who he

The 7 Spheres of a FriendMaker

had fallen out of relationship with over the years. None of his phone calls were intentionally about his business; he just called to say hi and to see how people were doing. He knew that if he was going to have the kind of business he wanted, he had to do the hard work of building the infrastructure of relationships that would help him to create the kind of momentum he needed to sustain a successful business in his community. He also knew that a lot of marketing is indirect rather than direct.

People don't want to be sold, they just want to be listened to, learned, liked, shown loyalty, leapt for, led, and loved! He had heard about Harvey McKay's concept of "dig your well before you're thirsty,"[38] so he began reestablishing old connections, networking with new people, and really befriending the people he had in his database. The attendees of the workshop had all become business partners and friends with him and each other. They even had a growing referral directory that they were all giving their clients to refer each other to. The phrase, "I need your help!" became a regular part of all of his conversations as he began to realize the power of asking people for their business, their referrals, and their support.

Nolan received a couple of referrals initially from his efforts of reconnecting and by the time six months was up, he had closed on three sales deals and had ten new transactions in his pipeline. Making friends was turning into profitable business.

One morning, he was busy handling several home inspection repair requests, getting ready to meet a buyer for a showing, and closing on a business deal all in the same day. He decided in the midst of his busy morning that he'd make a quick stop at The Bistro and grab a cup of coffee. As he walked up to the counter he looked over in the corner and saw Fran Lee and Dave Sawyer having a conversation over some cut up pineapple and eggs and toast. He remembered his conversation with Fran several months prior when he saw she was busy working her business and how much he'd envied that himself. Now he was in the same position, busy as ever with little time to stop for chit-chat.

Dave waved for him to come over, so Nolan got his coffee and walked over to their table. Fran said, "Pull up a chair, Nolan! I hear you've seen considerable growth in your business these last six months!"

Nolan blushed and quickly responded, "I can't talk long guys. I've got a lot going on today!" Nolan knew that he wasn't nearly as successful as Fran, but it meant a lot for her to compliment him so kindly. "Yes, I've been dwelling in the Seven Spheres with each of my clients and you know, my life is slowly but surely changing. My business is growing, and that's amazing. But something else has happened that I didn't realize."

"What's that, Nolan?" Dave asked.

"Well," Nolan continued, "The spheres are helpful in business, but I've been putting them into practice with my wife and kids, too. I've found that dwelling in these spheres with my family has really helped us all grow closer together. My wife appreciates that I spend time listening to her and learning who she is more deeply. As a result, we both like each other more than we used to. We actually enjoy spending time with one another. There's a real joy when we wake up in the morning that wasn't there before. All of this has served to increase our loyalty and faithfulness to one another. I would do anything for my family. The Seven Spheres have reminded me to leap and take risks for my wife and children because I want to lead and love them well.

"And I have found, with all of this, that our family operates much better together when we all dwell in the spheres together. Life is a little bit smoother and a whole lot more fun than it was six months ago. And I've got a little bit more money sitting in my bank account than I did be-

The 7 Spheres of a FriendMaker

fore, which has given us some financial security that we've just never had. Breathing room, you know?"

Dave and Fran were smiling from ear to ear. "Nolan, you've hit the nail on the head, my friend!" Dave exclaimed. "This was never about just a way to do business, it's always been about changing the way you do your life. Some folks come to my seminars looking for the secret ingredient to help them make more money. And some people leave my seminar unwilling to dwell in the spheres, unwilling to do the work that it will take to become the kind of person others want to do business with. But now you understand, Nolan. Business ownership is built on the foundation of real authentic relationships, true friends."

Fran chimed in, "You see it now, don't you, Nolan?"

Nolan smiled. "Yeah, I see it. Now I'm ready to see how many friends I can make!"

"Get after it, Nolan," Dave replied. "*Remember, he who dies with the most friends...wins!*"

"A Friend - True Friend - is someone who comes alongside you when you are broken, smiles with you when you are laughing and loves on you when you need it most. Art Kelly is my Friend."

Dave Sowards
Charleston, WV

Acknowledgements

Behind every great task there are always great people. I'd like to thank several people who have made this entire manuscript possible. Some of these people are friends from long ago and others are new friends I've made in recent months. All the rest are friends I've made all along the way and I'd like to take a few moments to acknowledge them. All of them are FriendMaker's through and through.

Rebecca. I've made mention of you once already, but I truly am thankful for you. You are my companion, my sounding board, my street smarts, and my very best friend. Thank you for letting me be your companion in life. These lessons haven't been easy to learn and would have been difficult had I no one to share them with. You've listened to me. You've seen me, known me, liked me, shown loyalty to me. You've taken a huge risk taking my hand and jumping into life together. You've served me as much as, if not more than, I've served you. And you continue to show your love to me consistently every day. I'm so glad you still care. Thank you.

The 7 Spheres of a FriendMaker

To my friends Chris, Lindsey, Brian, Amanda, Jacob, Meghan, Matt & Randi Lea. You are our companions along the road, our family community, and we have shared many years together. This is birthed out of our many interactions, our fireside chats, our beach conversations, and our life lived alongside of each other. Thank you, my friends. You are truly special to me.

To Jacob, Jeffrey, Mark, & Sam. Your brotherhood has carried me through so many highs and lows. I am grateful for you all. Thank you.

To the many family and friends who are too numerous to mention in my book but who have been along for the ride, I love you as well. Parents, siblings, friends and coworkers, this work comes from all of you who I've known for a short or long time. I am grateful.

To my business friends, Lesa Cegielski, Sean Carpenter, Rob Walls, Luke Jordan, Doug Austin, Chris Garrett and Brent Scott. You have been teachers and friends along the way. You've been some of my biggest cheerleaders and you've helped me get this thing off the ground. I'm grateful for your wisdom and for blazing a trail. Thank you.

To my publisher, Addis Press. Tyler & Cathie Quillet. You guys have been great. Thank you for believing in this project and in me and taking my passion and turning into a visually pleasing book and brand. I am grateful for our new friendship.

To my editor, Amber. Thank you for cutting my words down and challenging this wordy author to be more concise and precise with my words and ideas. I appreciate your work and your edits.

To you the reader. Thank you for taking the time to read my book. I hope it has challenged you to be a FriendMaker in your occupation, your business, your family, and your life. I can't wait to hear your stories.

FRIENDMaker

Endnotes

Introduction

1) Levins, Hoag. Social History of the Pineapple. [website: Levins.com] 1995-2009. https://www.levins.com/pineapple.html

2) The Pineapple Team. $8000 fuit: The Luxurious History of the Pineapple. [website: The Happy Pineapple Co.] January 30, 2021. https://happypineappleco.com/blogs/the-pineapple-blog/the-8000-fruit-the-luxurious-history-of-the-pineapple

How To Read This Book

3) Breen, Mike. Pp. 85-97. Building a Discipling Culture. 3DM International; 2nd Edition, 2014.

Part 1

4) Tidona, Christian [@tidona]. You want to know who your friends are? "Start your own business and ask for their support." ~Steve Jobs #entrepreneurship #friendship [Tweet]. Twitter. https://twitter.com/tidona/status/1307339426847219713?lang=en

The 7 Spheres of a FriendMaker

5) Alfred A. Montapert Quotes. (n.d.). BrainyQuote.com. Retrieved November 28, 2022, from BrainyQuote.com Web site: https://www.brainyquote.com/quotes/alfred_a_montapert_131276

6) Author Unknown.

Chapter 1

7) Tahmincioglu, Eve. September 7, 2006. Friends Don't Always Make Good Partners. New York Times. [website] https://www.nytimes.com/2006/09/07/business/07sbiz.html

8) Shapiro, Steve. p.4 Listening for Success: How to Master the Most Important Skill of Network Marketing. Chica Pubns; 1st Ed. 1999.

9) Bird, Drayton. (2020, September 11) Nothing happens in business until something gets sold." - Thomas J. Watson Jnr. CEO of IBM. [LinkedIn] https://www.linkedin.com/pulse/nothing-happens-business-until-something-gets-sold-thomas-bird/

10) U.S. Bureau of Labor Statistics Website data. Based on the average consumer spending in 2021 of $66,928 multiplied by estimated U.S Consumer Population of 139 million divided by 365 days the average consumer spending is $25,487,649,315. https://www.bls.gov/cex/tables/calendar-year/mean/cu-all-multi-year-2021.pdf

11) Ziglar, Zig. p. 201. Better Than Good: Creating a Life You Can't Wait to Live. Integrity Publishers. 2006.

Part 2

12) Eldridge, John. Pg 14. Epic: The Story God is Telling. Thomas Nelson. 2004.

Chapter 4

13) Aristotle. Book VIII, Section 3. Nicomachean Ethics. 350 B.C.E. MIT Internet Classics Archive online. http://classics.mit.edu/Aristotle/nicomachaen.8.viii.html

Part 3

14) Frost & Hirsch. p. 120. The Faith of Leap: Embracing a Theology of Risk, Adventure & Courage. Baker Books. 2011.

Chapter 5

15) Frost & Hirsch. p. 120. The Faith of Leap: Embracing a Theology of Risk, Adventure & Courage. Baker Books. 2011.

Author's Note

16) Buffini, Brian. (Host). May 28, 2019. Getting Things Done with David Allen #156. [Audio podcast episode]. The Brian Buffini Show. https://buffini.libsyn.com/getting-things-done-with-david-allen-156

Chapter 7

17) Kendall, Larry. Pp. 66-72. Ninja Selling: Subtle Skills, Big Results. Greenleaf Book Group Press. 2017.

Chapter 8

18) [Prowess] "Prowess means exceptional skill or ability. Your sailing prowess might save your life in a storm, while someone with less experience might make mistakes." © 2022 Vocabulary.com, Inc., a division of IXL Learning · All Rights Reserved. https://www.vocabulary.com/dictionary/prowess

19) Chandler, Steve & Rich Litvin p. 15. The Prosperous Coach. Maurice Bassett; Illustrated edition (April 30, 2013)

Chapter 9

20) Goenka, H [@hvgoenka]. (2020, February 20). People are like books - some deceive you by their glossy cover and others surprise you by their deep content. #FridayFeeling [Tweet]. Twitter. https://twitter.com/hvgoenka/status/1230727837847474176?s=20&t=UJ-ilErCCMBbtIWokdGyMQ

21) Burchard, Brendon. [@brendonburchard] (2022, January 14). Don't take yourself too seriously. Be the person who brings joy, humility and fun, even as you strive to reach difficult goals and make your difference. [Post]. Instagram. https://www.instagram.com/p/CYs68bFLTtk/?igshid=YmMyMTA2M2Y%3D

Chapter 10

22) Lange, Katie. February 22, 2011. There's No Whining in Real Estate – 2 Ways to Differentiate Yourself. Inman News web article: https://www.inman.com/next/theres-no-whining-in-real-estate-2-ways-to-differentiate-yourself/

23) Andrews, Andy. 2006. The Seven Decisions, Decision 1: The Responsible Decision. https://andyandrews.com/downloads/print/AA_SevenDecisions.pdf

Chapter 11

24) Millionaire Moveclub. (2022, January 28). Steve Harvey: "Loyalty has an expiration date..." [Video]. YouTube. https://www.youtube.com/watch?v=4iYW7-8zCNY

25) Carpenter, Sean. October 17, 2022. Compared to What? Weblog article: https://www.carpscorner.net/2022/10/compared-to-what/

26) Author Unknown. (2013, February 24). In a Time of Universal Deceit — Telling the Truth Is a Revolutionary Act. Quote Investigator. https://quoteinvestigator.com/2013/02/24/truth-revolutionary/

27) Edelman, Richard. 2020. 20 Years of Trust. https://www.edelman.com/20yearsoftrust/

28) Nightingale, Earl. 2009. The Progressive Realization of a Worthy Goal. Nightingale-Conant Corporation. https://www.nightingale.com/newsletters/356/

29) McManus, Erwin. Pp. 15-16. The Last Arrow: Save Nothing for the Next Life. Waterbrook. 2017.

Chapter 12

30) Shinagel, Michael. (July 3, 2013) The Paradox of Leadership. Professional Development: Harvard Division of Continuing Education. https://professional.dce.harvard.edu/blog/the-paradox-of-leadership/

31) ESPN [@espn]. (2014, April 29). "Excellence is the gradual result of always striving to do better." – Pat Riley [Tweet]. Twitter.

32) Adams, Linda. Gordon Training Website (Date Unknown) Article entitled: Learning a New Skill is Easier Said Than Done. https://www.gordontraining.com/free-workplace-articles/learning-a-new-skill-is-easier-said-than-done/

33) Adams, Linda. Gordon Training Website (Date Unknown) Article entitled: Learning a New Skill is Easier Said Than Done. https://www.gordontraining.com/free-workplace-articles/learning-a-new-skill-is-easier-said-than-done/

Chapter 13

34) Chapman, Gary. The Five Love Languages: The Secret to Love that Lasts. Northfield Publishing, Reprint Edition. January 1, 2015.

35) Clear, James. Pp 54. Atomic Habits: An Easy & Proven Way to Build Good Habits and Break Bad Ones. Penguin Random House USA; 1st Edition. 2019.

36) Clear, James. Pp 41. Atomic Habits: An Easy & Proven Way to Build Good Habits and Break Bad Ones. Penguin Random House USA; 1st Edition. 2019.

37) Walt Disney. (n.d.). AZQuotes.com. Retrieved November 29, 2022, from AZQuotes.com Web site: https://www.azquotes.com/quote/1055488

Epilogue

38) McKay, Harvey. Dig Your Well Before You're Thirsty. Currency by Doubleday. 1997.

IN THE SEVEN SPHERES OF A FRIENDMAKER WORKSHOP, YOU & YOUR TEAM WILL:

- Learn how to increase your productivity by focusing on first developing a plan for your own personal growth.

- Be challenged to do your work with excellence.

- Learn how build stronger client relationships by dwelling in the 7 Spheres of a FriendMaker.

- Increase your client retention.

- Learn the 7 core attitudes and 21 practices that will help you become the kind of person others will want to do business with.

- Get 21 lead generation ideas that you can use alongside the 7 spheres to get you solid business referrals within the next 90 days.

- A 1 1/2 - 2 hour interactive presentation by Art Kelly at your business office, conference space, or event.

- Each session comes with a downloadable pdf copy of the 7 Sphere's of a FriendMaker Workbook, and a copy of the book.

IF YOU WOULD LIKE MORE INFORMATION ON HOW THIS WORKSHOP CAN HELP YOUR BUSINESS, YOUR TEAM, OR YOUR COMPANY, EMAIL BOOKING@FRIENDMAKER.ORG OR VISIT HTTPS://FRIENDMAKER.ORG/SPEAKING#BOOK-NOW

Introducing the 7 Spheres of a FriendMaker Framework

the 7 spheres of a FRIENDMaker WORKSHOP

TRAIN YOUR TEAM TO BUILD THEIR BUSINESS RELATIONALLY BY HOSTING

ART KELLY

Company Trainer, Business Consultant, Coach & Realtor

- Increase your salesforce productivity by helping them develop a plan for their own personal growth.
- Challenge your sales force to serve clientele with excellence.
- Learn how to build stronger client relationships by dwelling in the 7 spheres of a FriendMaker
- Increase your client retention
- Learn the 7 core attitudes and 21 practices that will help you become the kind of person others will want to do business with.
- Learn 21 new lead generating ideas.

TWO WAYS TO BOOK ART FOR YOUR COMPANY TRAINING

E-mail booking at
booking@friendmaker.org

Register online at
www.friendmaker.org

TRAIN YOUR AGENTS AND SALES FORCE TO BE THE KIND OF PEOPLE OTHERS WANT TO DO BUSINESS WITH.

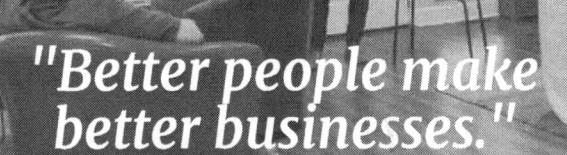

"Better people make better businesses."

Art Kelly

REVIEWS OF THE FRIENDMAKER WORKSHOP

DOUG AUSTIN
BENCHMARK REALTY, LLC
NEW AGENT TRAINING BROKER

We have over 1,400 agents here at Benchmark Realty. We host multiple company wide Mastermind meetings each year to engage, motivate, educate and inspire our affiliates. We brought Art on as our guest speaker to share his FriendMaker program and our affiliates loved it. Art did a great job keeping things fun and shared very real ideas that we can understand and implement immediately. If was refreshing, positive and very real. We have since had him back for multiple events both large and small.

BRENT SCOTT
OWNER
PREMIER HOME INSPECTIONS, LLC

Art has been demonstrating the "FriendMaker" concept in his business, personal life and and faith since I've known him. His presentation to my team was fantastic. He brought up great ideas and concepts that gave us conversation points about how to serve our clients better. It also helped us be open to how we can serve each other better. I highly recommend Art to anyone who has a team and is looking for ideas on how to grow together and want to build strong relationships with your clients. I look forward to having him back.

Made in the USA
Columbia, SC
27 February 2025